DEFENSE LAWYER CONFIDENTIAL

DEFENSE LAWYER CONFIDENTIAL

by
Alexander Y. Benikov

TWELVE TABLES PRESS
XII

www.twelvetablespress.com

P.O. Box 568
Northport, New York 11768

Library of Congress Cataloging-in-Publication Data

Name: Alexander Y. Benikov
Title: Defense Lawyer Confidential
Description: Northport, New York: Twelve Tables Press, 2017
ISBN 978-1-946074-16-4(print)/ISBN 978-1-946074-17-1(ebook)
Subjects: Law—United States/Criminal Law
LC record available at https://lccn.loc.gov/

Twelve Tables Press, LLC
P.O. Box 568
Northport, New York 11768
Telephone (631) 241-1148
Fax (631) 754-1913
www.twelvetablespress.com

Printed in the United States of America

Table of Contents

Foreword

I suspect that many believe that lawyers are simply made—a product of privilege whereupon completion of their first four years of partying through undergraduate school, their parents help finance the future lawyers' way through law school, and when they get their law degrees, the recent graduates decide which six-figure jobs they would like to accept.

I suspect that many believe that when newly minted lawyers accept this job, the new lawyers will have fancy offices and clients will just come to them or their firms with their cases and their money. Certainly, this may happen on occasion, but experience tells me that this is not always the case. In my mind, those of us who have lived a life outside of being a lawyer have the most insight and empathy toward our clients. Alex Benikov is a prime example of just such a lawyer.

As you read *Defense Lawyer Confidential*, you will come to understand that Alex is a lawyer who came from humble beginnings, who worked hard to not only get into law school, but also to become an actual practicing lawyer without having anything handed to him. In this book, you will learn about his background and his maturation as a lawyer through stories about his career that are both whimsical and thought provoking.

Furthermore, unlike what you see on television and in the movies, Alex's stories are real. They are not sensationalized to titillate the audience. Instead, these stories are compelling because they offer insight into the thought process of a criminal defense lawyer and those they represent.

I suspect that when you read these stories, you will come to view criminal defense lawyers and the people they defend differently. As Alex details in the upcoming pages, we are not the unethical individuals who are often portrayed on television or in the movies, but rather, criminal defense lawyers are law enforcement officers who enforce the Constitution.

We are the wall that stands between the power of the government and the liberty of each and every citizen in this great country. In this regard, I am proud to call Alex a fellow officer, and it is my hope that you enjoy reading his book as much as I did.

L. Kirk Nurmi, Defense Lawyer
Phoenix, Arizona

Chapter One

The Beginning

"Truth is stranger than fiction, but it is because fiction is obliged to stick to possibilities; truth isn't."

—*Mark Twain*

I once represented a woman who stabbed her husband in the head with a fork because he would not share his Italian food with her. When I asked her what happened, she told me exactly that. Welcome to the world of criminal defense.

One character trait that all defense lawyers share is a belief that everyone's rights have to be protected. I never met a defense lawyer who did not agree with this principle. All defense lawyers stand up for people who have no one else on their side. Whether the defendant is a child molester or a homeless person or a career criminal, the defense lawyer is the last line of defense when it comes to protecting people's rights.

Defense lawyers do not ask if their client is innocent or not. Defense lawyers fight every day to protect not only

their clients, but something all Americans claim to love—
the Constitution. If not for the attorney who represented
my parents when they had no one else on their side, I would
not be writing this book today.

Introduction

This book is a collection of stories from my years of
being a criminal defense lawyer. Like the work of a criminal
defense lawyer, the stories range from hilarious to tragic
and everything in-between. I wanted to write this book for
four main reasons.

First, I wanted to write this book for law students who
may be interested in going into criminal defense. Just like
a preview of a movie gives the viewer a glimpse of what
a movie is about and if it is worth seeing, I hope that this
book will serve as a preview of what being a criminal defense
lawyer is like. Too many students walk into this line of work
with false expectations and erroneous beliefs.

If a law student reads this book and says this is what he
or she wants to do with his or her career, then that is great.
Conversely, if law students read this book and say that this
is not for them, I am equally happy. We all have to choose
our own paths in life. My only goal is to give law students
as much information as possible about the world of defense
lawyers before they make their own decision. It is not my
goal to talk anyone into either becoming or not becoming
a defense lawyer.

Second, I wanted to write a book that new defense lawyers could use as a road map, not only in their new practice, but also in their careers. When I started my practice, a book like this did not exist. If a book like this had been around, it would have saved me a lot of worry and headaches. I hope the stories and experiences in this book allow new defense lawyers to learn from my mistakes, so they can avoid making the same or similar mistakes. I hope new defense lawyers use this book as a manual and refer to it often when issues or questions come up.

I remember being a new defense lawyer and not knowing up from down. I remember being scared and feeling like I knew nothing about being a defense lawyer. The information in this book will offer not only career and professional advice to new lawyers but also practical knowledge that will be useful during the everyday course of being a criminal defense lawyer.

The third reason I wanted to write this book is that there is an amazing amount of misunderstanding of not only the criminal justice system but also the work of criminal defense lawyers. Every defense lawyer knows this. Every defense lawyer has—at one point or another—been approached and asked: "How can you defend those people?" Every defense lawyer has been asked if he or she got someone off on a "technicality." Furthermore, every defense lawyer has had to explain that the "technicality" is the U.S. Constitution. I do not think that there is a single profession that is more misunderstood by the general public than the job of a criminal defense lawyer. If this book serves in small part as a defense of my profession, I will be happy.

Part of the reason that the criminal defense world is so misunderstood is because of the way defense lawyers are portrayed in popular culture. Virtually every popular book and TV show that has a defense lawyer character portrays him or her as being unethical and someone who cuts corners and does not follow the rules. Shows ranging from *The Sopranos* to *The Simpsons* all feature unethical lawyers.

On *The Simpsons*, the old corporate lawyer only wants to hurt the environment and is soulless and humorless. The other lawyer on *The Simpsons* literally chases ambulances. *The Simpsons*, like many shows, depicts lawyers as soulless bloodsuckers or outright clowns.

One of the most popular shows over the last couple of years features one of shadiest defense lawyer of all. Saul Goodman on *Breaking Bad* does everything wrong. Mr. Goodman lies, cheats, commits crimes, embezzles, and cuts every corner he can. When I teach Professional Responsibility, I actually play clips of the show to teach students what not to do. The problem is that many people watching the show think that this is what an actual defense lawyer is like. People watching the show know that Mr. Goodman is a fictional character, but he still resonates with people because they do not know any real defense lawyers, so they think there might be a reasonable amount of truth to the fictional character.

Many other shows depict lawyers as ethically challenged, and some show them as actual criminals. *The Wire* was one of my favorite shows, but the main lawyer on the show has not helped the public view of defense lawyers. He is actively engaged in committing crimes along with his drug-dealing clients and he seems to have little hesitation about his actions.

The phenomenon of how defense lawyers are depicted is not limited to TV shows and films. Pick up pretty much any John Grisham novel and you are likely to find a corrupt or unethical or unsympathetic lawyer character. I have read many John Grisham novels and rarely is there a lawyer who can be held up as a moral example.

I understand that the role of TV shows, movies, and books is to tell entertaining stories and not to depict realistic, balanced defense lawyers, or lawyers in general. My point is that people's perception of how defense lawyers are viewed is shaped by popular culture. I hope to present a more realistic depiction.

Lastly, many people are curious about the criminal defense world. When I tell people what I do, I always get a lot of questions. Many people only hear about criminal defense lawyers from the media and are curious if the actual job is similar to what they see in movies, books, and TV. I have joked with my wife that I was going to start giving a fake occupation at parties to keep people from asking me a million questions. My hope is that this book will give the reader a glimpse into my world.

My Journey

My parents had just arrived in America and they were already facing the possibility of being labeled criminals. My family immigrated from the former Union of Soviet Socialist Republics (USSR) to the United States when I was eight years old. My parents fled the former USSR with the same goal as all refugees—to give themselves and their son a chance for a better life. My parents got out of the former USSR with no connections, no money, and no plans. They moved to the other side of the world in hopes of finding something better than what was available in the former USSR. In America, we were poor and unsure of how we would get by and pay for rent. When my parents came to the United States, they had less than three hundred dollars to their name.

My dad was working three jobs and my mom was working two. My dad had gone from being a college professor to washing dishes, delivering pizzas, and building fences. My mom had gone from being a high school teacher to doing odd jobs for minimum wage. I was nine years old and babysitting my newborn sister because we could not afford a babysitter.

There was a Goodwill donation site near our apartment. It was a trailer where people dropped off their donations. At night, there was no one working at the site so people left their donations outside the truck. My parents would take items that had been donated, as they thought this was how the program worked. My parents did not know how to read English, so they could not read the signs posted on the van. If they had been able to read the signs, they would have known that it was illegal to take items from the donation site after hours.

One evening, my parents were cited for taking the donations and told to appear in court where they would face misdemeanor theft charges. Obviously, my parents were terrified. They had no money, could not speak the language, and were now facing criminal charges. When it was time for my parents to go to court, they went and had planned on trying to explain to the judge that they did not know they were not allowed to take items and that they would not have taken anything if they knew it was against the law.

When my parents came to court, they were assigned a public defender. They had no idea what a public defender was as there was no such concept in Russia. That public defender figuratively, and maybe literally, saved my parents. The public defender was able to get the charges thrown out, and my parents did not have a criminal conviction on their records. A criminal conviction would have likely kept them from getting many types of jobs. I never forgot what that public defender did for my parents. When I defend people today, I often think of that public defender and how he helped my parents in their time of need. That public defender had a large impact on my decision to go to law school.

My Law School Experience

I went back and forth on whether or not to include this section, but I decided to keep it as I think it is important that people, especially students who are financially struggling, understand what it takes to become a lawyer. If people understood the journey to becoming a lawyer, they may have more appreciation for the profession. I especially wanted to include this section for law students to know that they are not alone in struggling through law school. Law school simply opens the door to becoming a lawyer for law students. Law school does not decide if you will be a successful or unsuccessful lawyer. I am proof of this.

I always imagined that law school would be terrible. Before I could find out if my assumption was true, I had to get into law school. To get into law school, I had to take the LSAT. The LSAT is an all-day exam and is written by people whose whole goal is to trip up the test-taker by making the questions as confusing and difficult as possible.

I knew that in order to get into a decent law school, I would have to have a strong LSAT score. Most law schools use some combination of a formula to determine if they will admit you. Generally, the formula looks at your LSAT score and your undergraduate grade point average (GPA). I had really good grades in undergrad and in graduate school, but I had always struggled with standardized tests. Like most people, I took a prep class and studied hard (as hard as I studied before law school, which was not super hard compared to my studying habits while I was in law school). I took the test and did not feel great about it—but that was normal, so I was not too worried. The worry came into play when I received the results.

I remember the morning I received the results because I was going on vacation with my parents. To give you an idea of how I fared, a little explanation is needed as to what is a good score. The top score is 180 points. The Ivy League schools want scores in the high 160s and low 170s. Most state school law programs want a score in the low 160s or high 150s, depending on the school. I knew I would not be in the 160s but I was hoping for at least a 150. I got a 138. I might as well have received a letter stating: *PLEASE ABAN-DON YOUR DREAM OF LAW SCHOOL.*

I took the exam again several months later and did marginally better. I got a 145 on my second go-around. I applied to seven law schools and promptly received seven rejections. I did not even get a single wait list offer. For as long as I could remember, I had wanted to go to law school and now I was facing the reality that it may never happen.

I started applying for associate professor positions at community colleges since I had my master's degree. No one even called me back. At some point, I applied to be an FBI Special Agent. The agency not only called me back but flew me to Phoenix for an interview. I had made it more than half way through the selection process, and then they told me I had not made the cut. I could not find a teaching job, no law schools wanted me, the FBI did not want me, and I had no idea what I was going to do with my life.

At about this time, I remember receiving a flier from a law school called Thomas M. Cooley located in Lansing, Michigan. I looked up the school and saw that it was not ranked in the US News and World Report. I had no interest in moving to the Midwest, as I had never been there and I wanted to stay on the West Coast. I applied anyway, as I really had nowhere else to apply. Sometime later, I received a letter saying I had been accepted. For better or worse, I was moving to Lansing, Michigan.

Lansing, Michigan is one of those towns that became the focus of documentaries about what happens to a town when the automobile factories leave town. I could not really complain since the only law school that had accepted me was located there, so I did not have a choice.

When I flew to Lansing, everything I owned fit into two large suitcases. I was starting classes in January, so I flew to Lansing right before Christmas. The studio I had rented online was nothing short of terrible. The owners had done a good job of making it look livable in the pictures. As I stood on my balcony and looked at the view of old Oldsmobile plant, I feared this was an omen. I was going to attend a law school I knew nothing about and had never visited— while living in a state where I did not know a single person. My spirits were not high.

When I started classes, it was 2006 and the law school business was booming. My winter class (traditionally the smaller class compared to fall) had over four hundred students. At the time, Cooley was the largest law school in the country and had three campuses in Michigan. Two of the unique things common to first-year law classes is that you are told what classes to take, and second, you have the same people in all your classes.

The traditional first-year classes are some combination of Torts, Contracts, Property, and Criminal Law. It was easy to tell that some students would have a harder time than others. One student started taking the shrink wrap off his book to look inside it for the first time upon being called on to present a case. Another student asked if a dog could sue a person in court. The students were an interesting mix and so were the professors. Some of the professors were exactly what you would expect of law school professors—grumpy old white men who really enjoyed tormenting students for their own enjoyment, seemingly. Other professors were true teachers, mentors, and advocates of the law. The professors made school stressful, but the grades caused even more stress.

The old adage about law school is that in the first year, they scare you to death, in the second year, they work you to death, and in the third year, they bore you to death. The traditional approach was that once you make it through your first year, you did not really have to worry about getting kicked out because of grades. At my law school, people had to worry about grades during the entire three years. A lot of people were kicked out in the first year because of grades, but it did not stop there. I remember working as hard as I could and still being terrified for three years. Many of my friends did not make it.

Imagine not only being hundreds of thousands of dollars in debt, but also getting kicked out of law school and having no means to pay off those loans. I did not have a backup plan if law school did not work out. Luckily, things did work out and I graduated. However, this was where things would get really tough.

When I was nearly done with law school, I had the bar exam to look forward to. At Cooley, I took a bar exam prep course, and they showed us a graph. In the graph, you put in your law school GPA and your LSAT score, and the chart then gave you your estimated percentage of passing the bar. I suppose this graph was based on past bar exam takers. When I plotted my info, the graph told me I had a seventeen percent chance of passing. This meant I had an eighty-three percent chance of failing.

As I spent the next several months studying, I kept thinking about that seventeen percent. Knowing about the seventeen percent had a negative impact because it scared me and put doubt in my head. Conversely, it also helped because it motivated me to study harder, like the old cliché about excelling with a chip on your shoulder, about how you disprove doubters when no one believes in you. One of the recurring themes of this book is turning negatives into positives and turning a weakness into strength. I tried to turn the seventeen percent into a positive factor.

I took studying seriously and tried to take everyone's advice. Anyone who has ever taken the bar loves to give advice. Some of the advice is not great. Some was just plain terrible. One person told me not to study.

Some of the best advice that I received was to treat studying as a full-time job. This approach is nothing new, but very valuable nonetheless. Be at your desk on time in the morning and study all day with short breaks. I know for some people, studying full time is not an option, and I understand that and it may be how I beat my odds.

My single best piece of advice to law students is that you have to make time for studying or you are likely to fail. There are a few super-geniuses who can pass without studying. I knew I was not one of those people. My wife, then my girlfriend, was also studying for the bar, so she understood what I was going through. Having someone to study with was helpful. Even though we never actually studied together, I liked knowing that I was not going through everything on my own. Every day we complained to each other about how difficult the studying was and every day after complaining, we went back to studying. For nearly three months, all we did was study and go to our BarBri Bar Prep Classes. The long, tedious, and painful story made short—I passed the bar. I had passed by approximately one multiple-choice question, but I passed.

I had passed the bar and could not find a job. This brings us to my job at the bakery. I applied at the Maricopa Arizona County Public Defender's Office and was interviewed, but I was not offered a position. I thought that since I had interned at the Ann Arbor Michigan Public Defender's Office, I would likely get hired, but I was wrong. I had great letters from judges in Michigan and great letters of recommendation from my bosses in the Michigan public defender's office. None of the letters helped. I had sent out resumes and cover letters to every legal job I could find. I soon lost track of how many resumes I had mailed. I did not even receive one response thanking me for my interest. I contacted every Cooley Law School alumnus who I could find in the Phoenix area. I remember that I had a spreadsheet of alumnus that I had received from Cooley. I went down the list and contacted every single one. I felt like a telemarketer who was cold-calling people.

Many ignored my phone calls and e-mails. A few met with me and were helpful and gracious with their time, but no one offered me a job. They did not even know of anyone who was hiring. At that time, lawyers who had jobs were thankful to still be employed. One of the alumni who later became my good friend told me that he had a pile of over three hundred rejection letters when he was looking for work. I knew I was going to be fighting an uphill battle, but I do not think I had predicted how steep the hill would be. Most law firms were downsizing and laying off lawyers, and here I was trying to land my first legal job.

After I could not find a legal job, I began looking for nonlegal jobs. I was kind of picky about the type of job I wanted at first. I kept telling myself that someone *should* give me a good job. I thought I went through enough school, got my master's and my juris doctorate (JD), and passed the bar exam; all this *should* be enough and *I should* get a job. I had been in college and law school for eight consecutive years, and now I was done. I thought that attending school would ensure that I land a job, but I was wrong. After a couple of months of not working, I began to look for any kind of job I could find.

I began to apply at every place I could. I hit a low point during an interview at a questionable telemarketing operation; the interviewer had a cross tattoo on his face. He explained that they did not pay for the first month of work but after that, the earning potential was limitless. I then applied to be a bicycle taxi driver and a regular taxi driver. I actually got an interview to sell carpets. I remember how excited I was to get an interview for a minimum wage job because at least they were giving me a chance. Another low point was while I interviewed at a truck driving school. My interview was in a trailer. The interviewer asked me why I was applying there since I was a lawyer. I told him I simply needed a job. I also lied and said I did not want to be a lawyer. I figured it would help my chances of getting hired. It did not.

Eventually, I learned about an opening at a bakery. The reason I knew of the opening and ultimately got the job was because my friend knew someone who worked there. At orientation, I remember that the other new hires were very excited because they would be making more than minimum wage. At this point, I had been so bummed out from not being able to get a job that I was just happy to be working. I was officially employed as a bread truck loader.

I had my bar card in my pocket, and I was loading bread trucks in the middle of the night for eight dollars an hour. I would start my shift at 2:00 a.m. and finish sometime in the afternoon. I was so tired when I woke up that I once wore two different shoes to work. Most of my coworkers were either recent immigrants or had not finished high school. I was working in the bakery, as it was truly the only job I could find. I had graduated from law school, passed the bar exam, and could not find a job as a lawyer. As some of you remember, 2009 was the middle of what many described as The Great Recession, and unemployment rates were the highest they had been since the 1980s.

Here I was, loading bread trucks in the dead of summer in Phoenix, sweating through my shirt and thinking, "I am a licensed lawyer. Why am I working at a bakery?" While studying for the bar exam—and afterward—I applied for many legal jobs. At first I was picky, but I later applied anywhere I could. The one place I really wanted to work was in the public defender's office. I remember thinking about how much that public defender back in Portland, Oregon had helped my parents. I wanted to help others, as he did for my family.

I resented working at the bakery, and continued to send out as many legal resumes as I could. I remember constantly checking various websites in hopes that new lawyer positions would be posted. I posted so many profiles on job websites that I often lost track of where I already had a profile and what my password was. While working at the bakery, I began to plan the opening of my own law practice. I had entertained the idea for a long time and had done a lot of brainstorming. I was also fortunate to have taken a Law Office Management class in law school.

Over the next several months, the idea of opening my own practice became even more attractive. The more I grew to hate the bakery, the more I wanted my own practice. Almost every experienced lawyer I spoke to told me that it could not be done, and that I had to work for someone else first. As I said earlier in the chapter, one of the reasons I wanted to write this book is because I could not find a resource about becoming a defense lawyer when I needed it the most. I also wanted to tell young lawyers that opening your own practice right out of law school is possible— incredibly difficult, but possible. When I was researching how to start my own practice, I looked at a lot of law office management books. I could not find a book called, "*You Work in a Bakery but You Want to Have Your Own Practice; Here Is What to Do*," because that was what I needed.

I hope this book will serve as a road map for people who find themselves in a similar position.

After a couple of months at the bakery, management learned that I was a lawyer. I was approached and told that they wanted me to stay with the bakery and work my way up the corporate ladder. This was good news. I could crawl out from the inside of a bread truck but there would be a downside. I would be giving up on a law career for the foreseeable future. I had a choice to make.

I could play it safe and stay at the bakery, or I could open my own law practice in a city where I had zero connections, zero contacts, zero legal experience, zero clients, and zero savings! I quit the bakery on a Friday and started my own practice the following Monday. Starting my own practice did not feel scary as I really did not have anything to lose. If the practice worked out then that would be great. If not, I would be back where I started, which was no money and no law career.

How Fledgling Defense Lawyers Become Real Defense Lawyers

Most defense lawyers start out in either a prosecutor's office or public defender's office. The reason for this is simple and twofold. The first part of the reason is that those jobs are the most accessible to new lawyers. They hire more, as they generally need more people than private firms, so it is easier to get a job there versus at a private firm. Secondly, prosecutor's offices and public defender's offices are a great place to get experience.

Lawyers at both offices have large caseloads, which translates to a lot of experience. Prosecutors and public defenders must balance not only caseloads but also trials and other aspects of their jobs. Both offices also train their new lawyers, which is invaluable. Oftentimes, the offices are short-staffed because of budget issues, which means new lawyers are typically thrown into the deep end.

Being thrown into the deep end may mean handling a type of case that the lawyer is not ready for and has to learn on the fly. I have talked to many public defenders who have told me stories of being over their heads and having to learn. The upside of this approach is that young lawyers learn quickly and gain valuable experience.

Unfortunately for newly minted defense lawyers and prosecutors, not all offices are created equal and not all supervisors are strong managers. What I mean by this is that some prosecutor's offices and public defender's offices are terrible places to learn and teach terrible habits that lawyers will carry with them.

Oftentimes, the problem is the person who is running the office. Anyone who has ever worked in an office knows that the office takes on the personality of the person in charge. If the person in charge is kind and patient, the office will be the same way. If the person at the top is problematic, well, you get the idea.

I was lucky that I learned in an excellent office. Technically, I was never an employee but only an intern, but I learned many good habits at a small public defender's office in Ann Arbor, Michigan. It was a very small office of only about ten lawyers, but they were all there because they wanted to be public defenders who serve their community. They were all very experienced and believed in the work they were doing. Many of them could have started their own practices and made more money, but they viewed defending disenfranchised people as a calling that was more important.

The chief public defender in Ann Arbor had been there for decades and could have retired a long time ago, but he did not because he viewed his work as important to helping the community. When people asked him what he did, he replied that he was in law enforcement. Often, this would confuse people, as they only thought that the police were in law enforcement, but he would explain that he made sure that the police followed the law and enforced it fairly.

I have had friends who were not as lucky as I was. They started out in offices that did not treat their employees well and made the lawyers not want to be there. The practice of law is difficult under any circumstances but can become intolerable in a bad environment.

For example, I had one friend who worked in a prosecutor's office in which the supervisor would stand at my friend's door to make sure he was not one minute late. If my friend was even one minute late, there were repercussions.

You can see how this would not make for a pleasant work environment.

Another example involved a different friend of mine who worked in a prosecutor's office where the supervisor would listen to the audio and video recordings of trials to check for mistakes made by his prosecutors. If he was doing this to brand new prosecutors, this would be one thing, but this was not what he was doing. He would pull recordings of prosecutors with ten or fifteen years of experience. Lawyers who had more trial experience than he did were subjected to unjust scrutiny.

It is scary for new lawyers to start working in an office. It takes a while to figure out whether or not the environment is suitable. If the environment is extremely toxic, it may be easy to tell, but this is not always the case.

If you are a new lawyer or law student and you want to work at a public defender's office, remember what I said earlier. Not all offices are created equally. If you are trying to decide which office you want to work for, there are several things you can do to make sure you end up working in a good place. First, try to talk to as many lawyers who either work in that office or have worked there in the recent past. Recent is the key word because talking to a lawyer who worked in a given office twenty years ago will be useless to you. By talking to lawyers who currently work in that office or have done so recently, you should be able to get a pretty good sense of the office, and if you want to be a part of it.

If you do not already know some lawyers in a given office, get to know some. Call a few public defenders, introduce yourself, and ask them to lunch or coffee. Every public defender is busy, but you would be amazed how many of them will make time for you. Everyone remembers being a law student or new lawyer and most people will help you.

Some questions to consider asking current or recent employees:

1. How do you like working there?
2. How is your caseload?
3. What kind of training were you given?
4. How long would you like to stay with the office? (very important question)
5. How is the camaraderie in the office?
6. How is the pay and the benefits?
7. If they have left the office, why did they leave?
8. What advice do they have for new lawyers coming to that office?
9. How well does management treat the lawyers?
10. How much room is there for advancement?

Obviously some of these questions are more personal than others and some lawyers will not be open about the more personal questions. Some lawyers you speak with will give you almost zero information, whereas others will be incredibly open and candid. The more lawyers you are able to speak with from a given office, the better idea you will have of what it would actually be like to work in that office.

Some newly graduated lawyers start out in private practice. The traditional route for these lawyers is to get hired on at a firm. These lawyers face the same problems that lawyers in government offices do because they might get lucky and get hired at a great firm or they might get hired at an unsupportive, unpleasant firm. I have seen many of my own law students get hired at these types of firms.

The newly employed lawyer is often not aware of the firm's negative reputation and voluntarily walks into a bad situation. Other times, fledgling lawyers may know that they are walking into a bad situation, but they might be so desperate for work that they sign up anyway. As there continue to be more law school graduates and less job openings, this will continue to be a reality for many.

Problems for new lawyers who end up at bad firms are twofold. First, the new lawyers inherit the bad reputation of the firm. Other people, including other lawyers, assume that if you work for an unethical firm, you are also unethical. Whether this is fair or not, it is a reality. I have spoken to judges and prosecutors who have had a negative opinion of a young lawyer just because of where that lawyer happened to work for some time. I have had prosecutors tell me that they would not trust lawyers from certain firms because those firms had burned them in the past.

Second, the new lawyers learn bad habits from bad firms. Often, the young lawyers do not realize that they are learning bad habits, as there is no one to teach them good habits and how to fix mistakes.

I have taken my law students to court with me and they are often surprised that I do something in a very different way than the firms where they used to work as interns. I will explain that what their old firm was doing was unethical, and the students will be very surprised by this, as they did not know the firm was doing something wrong.

I once had the displeasure of watching a new lawyer turn into a bad lawyer because of the firm he had worked for. When I first met the lawyer, he had already been working at a bad firm for some time, but as he stayed with that firm, and I saw a lot of his bad habits grow. For example, I saw how poorly he communicated with clients, and since I knew the firm he worked for, I knew this is where he was learning those habits. He was always late to court and often rude to support staff. The prosecutors began to notice this over time, and his reputation was damaged beyond repair.

What Defense Lawyers (Actually) Do

I do not think there is a more misunderstood profession in the United States than the job of a criminal defense lawyer. I had a friend describe our jobs in the best way possible. My friend says that defense lawyers are car salespersons, trying to sell people Ferraris on Ford budgets. What he means is that defense lawyers are the middlemen between prosecutors and our clients. A client will always want no jail or prison time, and a prosecutor will always try to give the client more jail or prison time than they want. Joking aside, negotiating is a big part of what defense lawyers do.

As I mentioned, a prosecutor and a defendant will almost always want something different. It is not often that a prosecutor has asked my client to do something and the client has said, "Ok, I have no problem with any of that and I will do all of it." More often, the conversation goes something like this (an actual case of mine):

Client: "I don't want to do any jail time."
Prosecutor: "I am asking for jail on your case because you are charged with a suspended license, and you have 17 prior convictions for the same offense; you also have several DUI convictions, and at least two reckless driving convictions."
Client: "Ok, but I still don't want to do any jail."

I have had countless conversations with clients where I tell them that what they are asking for is impossible. I explain that either statutorily or for other good reasons, what they want is an impossibility. Sometimes, the clients believe me, but other times they do not. On many occasions, I have had clients tell me, "Well, you just need to try harder."

Another important part of being an effective negotiator as a defense lawyer is managing the expectations of your client. I have a defense lawyer friend who has been practicing longer than I have been alive. He tells me that when he meets with a new client, and without knowing anything about their case, he tells the client to expect a long prison sentence. The client naturally panics, and the lawyer says he will do everything he can to keep the client out of prison. After that, any result short of a long prison sentence leads the client to think that the lawyer is a genius. It is always smarter to promise less and deliver more than to do the opposite.

Every defense lawyer has had someone tell them that defense lawyers get people off on "technicalities." The classic lawyer response is that the technicalities they are referring to is called the *U.S.* Constitution. Defending the Constitution is arguably the most important role of the defense lawyer.

When I was interning at the public defender's office in Michigan, I had the same questions that most *non-lawyers* have about defense lawyers: How can defense lawyers represent people that they know are guilty? How can defense lawyers try to free people charged with horrible crimes? When I asked my supervisor at the public defender's office, he told me that often we are not only defending the individual but also the Constitution and people's rights.

Oftentimes, our clients are guilty, and our job is not so much trying to "get them off" but to make sure their rights are protected. These rights are guaranteed to them by the Constitution. What this means is that a defense lawyer has to watch over the police and the judges and the prosecutors to make sure everyone is doing their job and staying within their own constitutional limits.

One of the parts of my job that I enjoy most is knowing that I can affect how an officer does his or her job. If I have a DUI case and the officer does everything wrong, he knows he will be accountable for his actions when he testifies. If I point out his mistakes, he will learn from them and not repeat them. Conversely, if an officer does everything right the first time, he knows I won't be able to poke holes in his work when he is testifying. A good criminal justice system must have checks and balances to work. A defense lawyer, at his or her best, is a check on the criminal justice system.

Being a Defense Lawyer Is Not for Everyone

"Know thyself."

—Socrates

Being a defense lawyer is not for everyone. This is incredibly important so I will write it again: Being a defense lawyer is not for everyone. When I was a new lawyer, there was a young man who wanted to be a defense lawyer. He had a relative who was a defense lawyer, so he thought he could do it too. The only problem was that he was a terrible defense lawyer. It was not that he could not figure out the law or trial work, his problem was that he did not understand people and lacked empathy.

The young man was once talking to a young lady who had been charged with a DUI, and she was crying. She was crying because she was scared; she was scared because she might have to go to jail. The young man told her that she should not get in trouble and the DUI charge was her fault. This is what a defense lawyer should NOT do.

A good defense lawyer must have empathy. If a person does not have empathy, it will be very hard for him or her to be a good defense lawyer. Empathy does not mean lacking a critical eye, or being overly emotional, or believing everything your client tells you.

Some clients are harder to be empathetic toward than others, and defense lawyers should realize this. A reasonable defense lawyer is not going to have the same level of empathy for someone who rapes a little child than for someone who gets a DUI. Also, my clients lie to me all the time. This does not mean I stop caring about their cases or trying to help them. My job is to help my client and to get the best possible result. Part of my job is also to make the client less scared. Figuratively, and sometimes literally, I have to hold my client's hand through the process.

Having empathy means that you have compassion for your client and try to help. I know many excellent defense lawyers, and they are not all equally empathetic. Some are more so, some are less so, but none of them would ever do what that young man did. To the surprise of no one, that young man is no longer a defense lawyer.

Having a good sense of humor also helps. Most defense lawyers have a great sense of humor—not all, but most. I think a good sense of humor helps defense lawyers deal with all the horrible things that we encounter. Many people use comedy as a release valve from not only the stress of the job, but also the stress of dealing with representing people charged with horrible crimes.

I know a few defense lawyers who I can say with certainty have zero sense of humor, but they are few and far between. Most defense lawyers, including myself, will sit around and tell war stories over who had the funniest or worst case and laugh about it. Oftentimes, lawyers do not want to bring their cases home, so they discuss them with other defense lawyers.

The conversations will go something like this:

Lawyer 1: "You won't believe what my client did, he threw himself out of his own window."

Lawyer 2: "Yeah, that's funny but my client did something even funnier. She was arrested after drinking lamp oil."

Lawyer 3: "Yeah, those are ok, but my client tried to assault a cop with a dildo."

A good defense lawyer must be able to deal with stress because anyone who tells you being a defense lawyer is not stressful is lying to you. The job is stressful for many reasons. One reason is that a defense lawyer often holds people's fate in their hands.

I recently finished a case where my client was facing close to seventy years in prison. I have to know that if I make a mistake, it could cost my client most of his life. This is a lot of pressure and some defense lawyers do not deal with the pressure well. Oftentimes, the stakes are not as high as life and death but just as high to the client.

When I represent someone charged with a misdemeanor, they often know that if they go to jail, they will lose their job. Many of my clients are working-class people and missing a few days of work will result in termination. If they lose their job, they cannot pay their rent, put food on the table, and so on. When I am doing a trial for that person, I know that my client might lose everything he or she has, depending on the outcome.

Often—even when jail is not involved—the stakes might be very high. Imagine the stress a DUI lawyer feels when representing a pilot, a truck driver, or a taxi driver. The defense lawyer knows that how he or she handles the case could affect the rest of that client's life.

The job is also stressful because of the people. I will talk a lot more about difficult clients later on, but as you can guess, a large part of a defense lawyer's job is dealing with difficult people. Sometimes, the people are difficult on purpose.

I represented one client who engaged in frivolous lawsuits for fun. Although a normal person might have a hobby like golf or traveling, my client's hobby was filing frivolous lawsuits against government agencies. He was a court-appointed client and I was happy that I only had to deal with him once.

Other times, clients are unintentionally difficult. They may be scared, confused, frustrated, or just lost in the system. Dealing with clients brings us to our next chapter, the types of work for defense lawyers.

Chapter Two

Types of Work for Defense Lawyers

One of the benefits of being a defense lawyer is that there are many different career paths to pursue. The two main job types for criminal defense lawyers is private practice and government work. There are also job opportunities for defense lawyers to work as contract lawyers, teachers, and as judge pro-tems. The goal of this chapter is not to do an exhaustive analysis of different career paths, but to give the reader an idea of what is out there as far as job types for defense lawyers.

Private Practice

Being a defense lawyer in private practice is what most people think of when they hear that someone is a defense lawyer. It is hard to find hard numbers on the subject, but from my own experience, most defense lawyers in private practice today are either in solo practice or in small firms.

Out of the hundreds of defense lawyers I know, only a handful work at large firms and about seventy percent are in solo practice, with the remainder working in small firms ranging anywhere from two to ten lawyers. If you are interested in working in a big firm, it does not mean you cannot do criminal defense. You just have to know that there will not be a lot of opportunities as most big firms do more civil than criminal work.

Being a defense lawyer in private practice means you eat what you kill. In other words, if you do not bring in clients, you will go out of business. This is both a positive and a negative aspect of private practice. The positive is that there is the opportunity to make a lot of money. I know some lawyers who are wonderful at marketing and have built incredibly successful practices. The negative is that if you are not good at marketing and bringing in clients, you will starve. I know many who are excellent lawyers but terrible business people and they can barely afford to keep the lights on. This goes back to the Socrates quote about knowing yourself. If you do not want to hustle and build up a client list, avoid private practice.

By all accounts, making a comfortable living today is harder than it has ever been in the past. Every defense lawyer friend of mine tells me that it was easier to get private clients ten or twenty years ago than it is today. There are many reasons as to why this is, but I think the biggest reason is market saturation. Even with the current decline in student enrollment, there are too many lawyers fighting over a piece of the same pie. As there are more and more lawyers, there are fewer cases to go around. Firms with large marketing budgets obtain a lot of clients and everyone else has to fight over the scraps. It is hard to tell what the market will be like in years to come but I can tell you that today there is a huge amount of competition for clients if you are a defense lawyer.

When I talk to my older defense lawyer friends, they tell me that getting clients used to be easy. One friend told me: "When I started my practice I plugged in my phone and it started ringing, I didn't have to advertise, the clients just showed up." This was twenty years ago and today, the reality is very different. If you are a lawyer starting your own criminal practice today, you have to be able to find clients. If you work for someone else, he or she needs to have enough clients to keep you busy. If there is not enough work to go around, I am sure you can guess what happens to your job.

Some lawyers think that if they are in a small market, getting clients will be easier. This is partially true. It is true that there will be less lawyer competition. The downside is that although there is less lawyer competition, there are also fewer cases to go around. If you live in a town of ten thousand people, how many DUI cases do you think there annually as opposed to if you are in a town of one million people?

One of the most common questions that my law students ask me is what is the average salary for a defense lawyer in private practice? As you may be able to guess, there is no average salary. There is a wide spectrum. According to Payscale.com, the median salary for defense lawyers in the United States in 2017 was just under eighty-one thousand dollars.[1] Here in the greater Phoenix, Arizona area, where I practice, I know some defense lawyers in private practice who make less than fifty thousand dollars a year and I know some lawyers who make well over half a million dollars a year. I am sure a defense lawyers in large markets like New York or Los Angeles can make even more money. Conversely, lawyers in very small markets earn less.

As I mentioned, when you are in private practice, you dictate your own income. This is a double-edged sword. If you are excellent at marketing and work harder than everyone else, you will make more than the lawyer who does nothing, is lazy, and sits by the phone waiting for it to ring. There is no magic to succeeding in private practice.

Public Defender

A large number of criminal defense lawyers start their career in a public defender's office. This is expected. Getting

---

1. http://www.payscale.com/research/US/Job=Criminal_Defense_Lawyer/Salary

a job at a public defender's office is much harder today than it was in the past. As there are more and more people graduating law school, there are less and less jobs available. Public defenders' offices are no exception, as today they receive more applicants than ever. Today, it is not uncommon to have over one hundred applicants for each spot. Public defenders' offices are also constantly dealing with tightening budgets. As budgets get tighter, there are less and less available positions.

The second interesting thing happening with public defender's offices is that more and more lawyers are leaving private practice to go back to the public defender's office. In the last several years, I personally know a handful of defense lawyers who gave up their private practice to go back to the public defender's offices. The two main reasons for this are both income related. As mentioned, making a living in private practice criminal defense is harder than ever. Some lawyers do not want to or are not able to keep fighting to obtain private clients. Some lawyers are choosing to go back to the steady paycheck they receive at the public defender's office.

The second reason is related to insurance. Anyone who has ever had to pay for his or her own health insurance knows how expensive it is. As some lawyers are having a hard time making money, they are not able to afford health insurance for themselves or their families. For some lawyers, going back to the public defender's office is worth it for the health insurance alone.

Contract Lawyer

The third main employment opportunity for defense lawyers is a hybrid between private defense work and a full-time public defender position. Being a contract defense lawyer is exactly what the name implies. You serve as a defense lawyer in a contract capacity with either a court, or a city, or any other agency. The reason that being a contract defense lawyer is a hybrid of a traditional public defender and a private defense lawyer is because you are serving, in part, both roles.

As a contract lawyer, you are still taking on private cases just like any private defense lawyer. The difference being is that you are having cases assigned to you as part of a contract. There are many different types of contracts available for defense lawyers. The contracts vary in pay, caseload, type of work, and many other ways.

The first contract case I ever did was for the local county superior court. The county had a contract that was essentially an overflow contract. If there were not enough public defenders, the county would go to the overflow list and ask the lawyers on that list if they wanted the case. This was a major felony contract list and I was still fairly new to criminal defense, so I was excited for the opportunity. The case I was assigned gave me a great way to learn and allowed me to make some money. I also always enjoyed knowing that if I worked hard, I would be able to help my clients. Many of my court-appointed clients never expect much from court-appointed lawyers; therefore, when they see you working hard, they are pleasantly surprised. The reason many clients do not expect much from their court-appointed lawyers is because many have had their own bad experiences, whereas others have heard stories from friends and relatives.

The next contract I held was at a city public defender's office. This city does not have a traditional public defender's office where the lawyers in that office work full time in the court. This city awarded contracts to defense lawyers for a period of one year. Under the contract, the lawyer was responsible for two pretrial days a month and any trials they set. I had this contract for five years and learned an incredible amount about defense work. Most of the lawyers working on the contract had substantially more experience than I had. There was one lawyer who had been practicing longer than I had been alive. While I had the contract, he celebrated fifty years of practice.

Some contracts hire defense lawyers to serve as what is known as advisory counsel. This means that the defense lawyer is there to help answer questions and give legal advice, but that lawyer is not actually assigned to the defendant's case. Most often, advisory counsel is present in jail court where he or she meets with defendants who have just been arrested. The benefit of working as advisory counsel is that you get to deal with a lot of people in a short amount of time, which is a great way to learn. I remember working as advisory counsel and talking to forty or fifty people in several hours. Some courts will also have advisory counsel present in arraignment court where defendants show up to make their initial appearance.

One other type of contract work that is available to defense lawyers is appellate contract work. With these contracts, a defense lawyer is appointed for appellate purposes and is paid per appeal. Some defense lawyers like these contracts because they do not have to go to court as most of the job is reviewing the trial transcripts. Some defense lawyers really like these contracts as they enjoy appellate work. I have always preferred being in the courtroom, so I shied away from appellate contracts.

The pay scale and pay structure of the contracts vary greatly. Some contracts pay a flat fee monthly. This means you could get only a few cases assigned or a lot and you would still be paid the same amount. Most contracts that pay a flat fee will try to keep an even caseload, but obviously there will be more cases during some months. The good thing about these types of contracts is that you know exactly how much you will be getting paid every month. The downside is that there is no opportunity to make more than the contracted amount.

A second type of contract pay structure is one that I generally prefer, and is one where the defense lawyer is paid per case. As you can guess, the major benefit of this type of contract is that if you get assigned a lot of cases, you make more money. Most courts with this type of structure will pay per case even if one defendant has more than one case.

I have had defendants who had eight or nine open cases and I got paid on each one.

The last type of pay structure for contract work is where the defense lawyer is paid hourly. Some of these contracts will have a cap on how many hours a defense lawyer can bill on a case, whereas others have no cap. Some of these contracts will even pay for travel time. For instance, you are appointed to a case where the client is in a prison two hours away. The drive there and back with a contract that pays for travel means you just billed four hours for driving.

The most common question that I get from law students and new lawyers is: How do I get a contract? The answer, like most things in life, is that you have to know the right people. If you do not know the right people, your chances of getting a lucrative contract are close to zero. The reason that you need to know the right people is twofold. First, you need to know the right people simply to learn what contracts are out there. Many of these contracts do not advertise at all and if someone does not tell you about them you will never know they exist. Second, you need to know the right people so they can vouch for you.

I got my first contract because I had done a lot of work in that court and had gotten to know the lawyers who had the contract. When the contract opened up, those lawyers vouched for me, which helped me enormously. By working in that court, I also came to know the contract administrators. When I applied, I was not just a name in a pile of hundreds of names. The contract administrators knew me, knew I would do a good job, and, most importantly, knew I would not make their lives more difficult if they hired me.

The second contract was with a judge I had appeared before hundreds of times over several years. He told the other people on the panel that he knew me and that I was competent. I just sat there at my own interview while the judge told the panel they should hire me. As of 2017, I have been in that judge's courtroom for over five years and recently spoke, at his request, at his reappointment hearing. Again, being a balanced, empathetic, self-aware individual might be your biggest advantage in building your practice successfully for the long term.

I tell you this not to make myself sound great, but to stress the importance of always showing respect, and, of course, knowing the people in charge. If you apply for a contract and you do not know the people in charge, or the decision makers, then you are not setting yourself up for success. Never forget the importance of treating everyone with respect and knowing the right people, and having those people like you. The practice, and the business of law has always been, and always will be, a people business. If you learn nothing else, learn this.

Judge Pro-Tem

If you do not know, a judge pro-tempore ("pro-tem") is a substitute judge. The regular judge could be on vacation, sick, or not available on a given day. Other courts use pro-tem judges when they have too many cases and need another judge. Some courts use pro-tem judges so much that a given pro-tem judge may be in a given court almost as much as the regular judge. Being a judge pro-tem is a great way to build your resume, especially if you are interested in becoming a regular judge down the road. Getting hired as judge down the road is easier when you have experience working as a judge. Being a judge pro-tem is also a great way to learn and build out your expertise.

Most judge pro-tem positions are paid. Many of the paid positions are hourly, whereas some pay for half day or whole day. Some courts ask the judge pro-tems to volunteer their time. Generally, I am not a huge fan of working for free but if the unpaid position is in a court where you want to make connections, or are interested in being a judge, then working as an unpaid judge pro-tem can be a great experience. Different courts have different standards for how long you have to be in practice before you can apply to be a pro-tem.

Some pro-tem positions are unpaid. I currently serve as a judge pro-tem in the Maricopa County Superior Court where I handle various criminal matters. Even though this position is unpaid, it is still fairly highly sought after. The position is great for people who are interested in becoming regular judges down the road as it shows potential employers that you have experience as a judge.

Teaching

There are many benefits of having a teaching position as a lawyer. One of the obvious benefits is having an extra source of income. Different teaching positions pay different amounts, but almost all of them pay something. When you are a new defense lawyer or having a difficult financial time, having an extra income from teaching could be the difference between staying afloat and going under. Another potential benefit is an extra source of referrals.

I have taught at the law school level for about five years and I have obtained many private clients from my students referring people they know to me. My students know I am in private practice so when they have a friend or relative who needs a defense lawyer, they think of me. I have had students refer everyone from their hair dresser, to their kids, to their employees. If you are teaching, make sure you respect your students because they are your future peers, and it never hurts to have the students know what you do and that you welcome their referrals. If your students do not know you take on private cases, how will they know to refer someone to you?

Another benefit of teaching is the professional opportunities that teaching can open up for lawyers. Through my teaching, I have had opportunities to speak at national and international conferences. I also landed my first book deal as a result of a class I was teaching. I have been fortunate to be able to write three law review articles as a result of teaching, working with passionate colleagues, and hoping to inspire students to not give up their dreams.

Although the most common and most traditional place for lawyers to teach is law school, there are also other options. I know several lawyers who teach in college programs. Several others teach in paralegal programs. The nice thing about many of these programs is that they are now taught online, which means scheduling and teaching can be flexible. With online learning, a lawyer can work as a lawyer during the day and then teach online in the evenings or on the weekends.

Chapter Three

The Clients

All clients are unique, but after practicing long enough you notice that there are select types of clients. Some clients have similar personalities, whereas others have similar reasoning for doing what they do. The following list of client types is by no means exhaustive, but simply the types of clients I have come across the most often.

First Timers

Arguably, the most common type of client for any lawyer is the first-time client. Chances are high that this client is not a lifelong criminal, as most career criminals tend to get caught from time to time. First-time criminal defense clients can go one of two ways: the easy way and the hard way.

The easy way happens when they trust their lawyer and take their advice. The hard way happens when they are so new to everything that they do not know what they should be scared of and will often try telling their defense lawyers what to do.

When I deal with first-time clients, there are several things that I have to keep in mind. First, everything is new for these clients, and they are likely scared. They are scared of what will happen with their case. They may be scared of how the case will end, or what the outcome will be. Oftentimes, these clients are scared of the whole judicial system, regardless of whether their case is criminal or civil.

Sometimes, with first-time clients, I have to be prepared to explain everything in great detail. I may have been in a given courthouse a million times, but for these clients, it is their first time. They are nervous about where to sit, what to do, what the judge will say and do, and so on. These clients are paying you to make them feel more comfortable and to explain everything. Remember that just because the clients may not be visibly nervous does not mean that this is the case.

Another consideration for first-time clients is that they may require more "hand-holding." I have had older clients who would literally hold my hand before walking into court. The hand-holding may range from answering more questions to just explaining things in more detail than you are used to. Generally, these clients will want or need more hand-holding, not because they are trying to be difficult, but because they are scared and/or nervous.

Some of my best and worst clients have been first-time clients. I represented a young woman once who, to this day, is one of my favorite all time clients. She was charged with a DUI, but her blood alcohol content was relatively low, just over the legal limit. We had a long trial and the jury eventually convicted her. After the verdict, she gave me a hug and said that she has never had someone work as hard for her.

A different female client was one of my most-difficult-to-work-with clients. The woman had been charged with reckless driving, criminal speeding, and a few other moving violations. The police had been following her on the highway and had videotaped her as she was swerving in-between lanes while going eighty miles per hour, and putting on makeup. The woman had twenty-two speeding tickets in the last three years. The tickets were all civil, so she had never been to criminal court.

I represented her for months and the whole time, she kept telling me she was innocent. I told her that we could take the case to trial but that the video would speak for itself. She thanked me for all my hard work by firing me from her case. She was convicted of all charges soon after, under the representation of her new counsel who I am sure represented her professionally and patiently.

Frequent Fliers

The second type of common client is the opposite of the first-time client and is often referred to as a frequent flier. This type of client has used or needed the assistance of lawyers on numerous occasions.

If you are a lawyer who does a lot of felony work, you will have a lot of these clients. People who have been in trouble their whole lives are no strangers to lawyers. Some clients may have had over ten lawyers in the past several years. What this means for you when you represent them on their fifth felony is that these clients will know their way around lawyers. Worse yet, they will think they know the law.

One potential issue with frequent fliers is that they will think they know everything and will often think they know more than you. When I was new to felony work, I found that the defendants who had been in the system for so long actually did sometimes know things that I did not. The problem with clients who think they know everything is that they make your job more difficult. They are more likely to second guess you at every turn and try to tell you how to do your job.

One positive aspect of frequent flier clients is that they are not as scared as first-time clients. Frequent fliers will usually require less hand-holding. A felon who has been to prison on several occasions will know what to expect from prison and will be realistic about the possibilities or returning there. I have had several clients who told me they preferred being in prison to being free. Which of the following two clients will be more demanding of your time and which one will require more hand-holding? A client who is looking at six months in prison but has never been to jail, or the lifelong felon who has spent a total of twenty years in prison and is looking at two more years? As always, there are no ironclad rules. You can probably guess the defendant looking at six months will be more scared and need more hand-holding. The following hypothetical is based on an actual client I represented. It also happens to be the first major felony case I had handled. Frequent flier clients often have the best explanations.

I represented a man who was arrested and while being searched incident to arrest, drugs were found in his pants pocket. He told the police that he had been at a pool party the night before and everyone got naked and went swimming. He then explained that he had accidentally put on someone else's pants so the drugs were not his. As you can imagine, the client realized that this story was not very believable and ended up pleading guilty.

I had another defendant who was arrested for a DUI. While searching the car, the police found a ski mask, a gun, a scale, and drugs. The defendant had reasonable explanations for everything. The ski mask was because he liked to go hunting and did not like for his face to get cold. The drugs were lying on the ground and he picked them up because he did not want a kid finding them. The scale belonged to his mom and he was taking it back to her house. And the handgun? Obviously, that was for hunting also.

I had a frequent flyer case when I had been practicing on my own for less than one year. It would become a memorable case as I learned a lot about being a defense lawyer.

My client was out on parole after having just served ten years in the Department of Corrections ("DOC"). My client was fairly young, so he had essentially grown up in the DOC. The first thing my client did upon being released was commit several armed robberies. My client and his friend would walk into businesses, wave guns around, and demand money. They were also using a stolen car.

The prosecutor's case against my client could not have been stronger. The police not only possessed filmed confessions of my client, but also filmed confessions of his friend saying that my client was the mastermind. The prosecutor also had all the victims from the robberies who had identified my guy. On top of everything, the police found the video surveillance tapes from the businesses at my client's house.

The choice my client had to make was whether he would sign a plea agreement to serve the next twenty years of his life in prison or go to trial where he would be looking at life. The reason that my client could get so much more time if he went to trial was because the mandatory minimums on his charges could be stacked on top of each other. Instead of doing twenty years, he could have received three twenty-year sentences and ended up serving sixty years. This is one of the risks defendants with felony charges face when they proceed to trial. If my client signed the plea, he would get out when he was fifty. The prosecutor had added in the agreement that he could not get released early for good behavior, and he must serve the whole twenty years.

What surprised me about my client was how honest he was with his situation. He did not blame anyone else and took responsibility for his actions. I asked him if there was anything about his childhood that would be a mitigating factor for me to take to the prosecutor.

Sometimes, a prosecutor will give a better plea if the there is a good reason to do so, for example, if the suspect was abused as a child or grew up in a violent home. My client told me that he had great parents and had chosen the lifestyle, and it was not anyone's fault but his own. He signed the plea, and as of this moment that I write this, he has about fifteen years left to serve.

Clients with Mental Health Issues

I was in jail court recently (which is exactly what it sounds like) and there was a defendant who was yelling at the judge. The defendant claimed that the judge was guilty of conspiracy to overthrow America and that the punishment was death.

The first thing to understand about clients with mental health issues is that they cannot be clumped into one category. There are thousands of mental health conditions, ranging from mild to severe. Also, two clients with the same diagnosis could be dealing with it in two very different ways. You could have two clients who are bipolar and one could seem completely normal, whereas the other may not be able to hold a conversation.

A good defense lawyer must know if the client has mental health issues for several reasons. First, you may have to make special accommodations to help the client. You will not know what accommodations to make if you do not know what issues your client has. The second reason is that it may affect how you handle the client's case. One of the courts I practice in has a special mental health court. The court may be able to resolve cases while getting clients the help they need.

Sometimes, it will be obvious that the client has mental health issues. I once represented a defendant who took a bunch of peanut butter and smeared it into his long hair. The transport officers brought him from the jail to the court, and he explained to me why he covered his head in peanut butter. I do not remember the exact explanation, but it had something to do with preventing the aliens from yelling at him.

Other times, it may be hard to tell if your client has any mental health issues. Sometimes, you may have a suspicion but may not be sure. Yet, other times the client may seem completely normal at first, but over time it may become clear that there are mental health issues. I had a client several years ago that demonstrated how this happens: The defendant seemed normal at first and had met me several times. Over time, as the client got to know me, he began to open up. When he opened up, he explained that dolphins were listening in on his thoughts, and it was hard to sleep. Just because there are no obvious issues at first does not mean there will not be issues later.

No one is expecting the lawyer to be an expert in diagnosing mental health issues. Lawyers are not trained in mental health and no one expects them to be. If you suspect your client has mental health issues, the best way to find out is to ask. I have had hundreds of defendants with mental health issues, and they almost never mind you asking them if they have mental health issues.

Obviously, you want to ask as gently and politely as possible. However, there is nothing wrong with asking. Say something along the lines of, "In order for me to represent you to the best of my ability, I need to know what your diagnosis is." Feel free to remind the client that what you are told is protected by privilege.

What do you do if the client will not or is not able to tell you? You may want to refer your client to a doctor who specializes in mental health and who can tell you if there are issues present. The doctor may also confirm your own suspicions and explain a medical condition that you may not understand or may not be familiar with. This is important for the prosecutor and the judge to know.

Another group of people you may be able to get answers from is the client's family. The family will know more about the issues the client has and can fill you in. Remember, you need the client's permission before disclosing anything to the family. Sometimes, the client will not want you to tell the family anything, and you are bound by those wishes.

I have had many memorable clients with mental health issues, but two really stick out in my mind. Both were very difficult clients but for different reasons. Both clients suffered from very vivid hallucinations and saw and believed many things that were simply not there.

The first client had been charged with harassment when he kept sending threatening messages to someone he thought was his girlfriend. He told her many strange things but one of the strangest was that he knew she was sleeping with President Obama (when he was the President). The woman eventually called the police, and he was charged with harassment.

The defendant had been previously charged with aggravated assault and was still dealing with that case. When I met with the client, it was very apparent he had mental health problems. He told me that he not only knew his "girlfriend" was having an affair with the President, but he could prove it through a Sudoku puzzle.

The second client's case was even more bizarre. I knew the client was going to be incredibly difficult since I was his third public defender. The first two had found him too difficult to deal with, and he was pawned off to me as a "special assignment." Looking back at the case, he was probably the single most difficult client I have dealt with.

The defendant had been charged with calling in death threats to a police station. The defendant had a long and colorful history of not liking the police. The defendant would call the police and say that someone was going to poison everyone in the station. He said the culprits were two women and that they worked at a bank. He gave the women's names and the name of the bank they worked in. The suspect also told the police that the two women belonged to several violent gangs.

When the police went to go talk to the two women, it was clear that the women had no intention to poison anyone and had never been in trouble with the law. It was also clear that the women did not belong to any gangs. The women asked if, by chance, the person who called in these threats was a former client of the bank. The women described the man, and it was the same person who was calling in the threats.

The women explained to the police that the person had tried to cash forged checks at their bank, and they would not give him cash since the checks were obvious forgeries. They not only refused to cash the checks, but also they informed the police of this situation, and the suspect was arrested on check fraud charges.

The police soon pieced together the whole picture. My client was mad at the two women and blamed them because he got caught with his check scam. He was now trying to get them in trouble with the police by trying to get the police to arrest the two women for making threats.

When the police arrested the suspect, he wrote a full confession. The police also seized the phone and obtained the phone records proving the threatening calls were made from my client's home. My client was also on felony probation due to the check charges, and he made a full confession to his probation officer at the police station. Later on, my client would claim that the police had broken into his apartment and made the threatening phone calls to themselves just to get him in trouble.

There were many strange things about the case, but the strangest aspect might have been that the suspect was found competent to stand trial by three different psychiatrists. The trial was very short, and my client was convicted. He not only appealed the decision but also filed an Ineffective Assistance of Counsel claim against me, saying I had not done a fair job representing him.

I think the most important thing I can tell you about clients with mental health issues is that they want to be treated like any other client. Treat the client respectfully and as normally as you can. Never talk down to the client or be mean. I am always amazed and saddened when I see a lawyer talking down to a client with mental health issues. Treat your clients as normally as possible, and they will appreciate it.

The last thing to mention is that, in my experience, clients with mental health issues are often easier to work with than regular clients. Out of the hundreds of mental health clients I have had, only a few have been difficult. I am not totally sure why this is, but it is true. Do not assume that just because you have a client with mental health issues that he or she will be difficult or unreasonable.

Angry Clients

Several months ago, I had a defendant who had been taken into custody. When I showed up to the jail, we had the following conversation:

Me: "Hello, I have been hired to represent your case and I will try to help you."
Client: "Go fuck yourself."
Me: "Ok, good talking to you."

A good defense lawyer must be realistic that there will be angry clients. There is no avoiding this. Thinking that you will not have angry or upset clients is like sticking your head in the sand. Once you accept that angry clients are a normal part of being a defense lawyer, it becomes easier to deal with such people.

Angry clients can be broken down into two main groups. The first group is actively angry clients. These are the clients who are angry and hostile from the first time you meet them. Often, these clients will be hostile toward you and anyone else involved in the case. They may not only be mad at you but also at the prosecutor, opposing counsel, judge, and anyone else involved in their case.

The second type of angry client is more subtle. The passive–aggressively angry client may not be as visibly angry but may be even more difficult to deal with. These clients may seem fine on the surface while doing passive–aggressive things that make it more difficult to represent them.

As the lawyer, you must realize that these clients are usually not angry with the lawyer. Angry clients are usually mad about everything in their lives. They are often mad at their marriage, their job, their finances, and anything else you can imagine. Oftentimes, inexperienced lawyers will not realize this and blame themselves for these clients' anger.

Do not think you are responsible for their anger. Chances are high that these clients were angry long before they came to you, will be angry while you represent them, and will be angry after you represent them.

The job of a defense lawyer is not to fix all the sources of anger in these clients' lives. Your job is to help with the specific task you are hired or appointed for. If a client hires you for a DUI, that is your only task. Your task is not to fix their failing marriage or to find them a better job. You are not a psychiatrist or a social worker. Too many lawyers think they are social workers, which is a big mistake.

Sometimes, angry clients become confrontational. Different defense lawyers deal with this in a variety of ways. A defense lawyer friend of mine who used to be a welder before going to law school had a very angry client. When my friend was working as a welder, his coworkers would have fist fights over the slightest transgression. When the client threatened my friend, my friend was not scared or even surprised and did not back down. The client soon realized that he had threatened the wrong person and sat back down. Getting a good read on clients is an art form. Be sure to know yourself and read your clients well.

Overly Emotional/Train Wreck Clients

Originally, I was going to have these clients have two different sections, but then I realized that they belong together. The reason is that it is almost impossible to have a train wreck client who is not overly emotional. Almost every emotional client will be a train wreck.

An overly emotional client can take a million different forms. They can be any age, gender, and race. It may be a client who cannot stop crying and cries throughout every court date. An overly emotional client can also be composed in court but become overly emotional when realizing the potential consequences of a given legal action. There is no easy way to define someone who is overly emotional.

If you are always reserved and you have a client who is less reserved than you are, you may consider the client overly emotional. If you are a very emotional person, you may consider someone who others see as very emotional as acting perfectly normally just because they are similar to you. The point is that one lawyer's overly emotional client is another lawyer's dream client.

I think the key to dealing with overly emotional clients is to remain calm and to carry on like there is nothing wrong. If you have a client who cannot stop crying and you start crying with them, will that help the situation? Just as with any type of client, you are there to do a job. Just because the client is or becomes overly emotional does not mean you do not have a task in front of you. There is nothing wrong with comforting the client, and often this will help the client calm down.

Train wreck clients are exactly what they sound like. Their entire lives are composed of a series of messes. They are running from fire to fire, trying to put them out but never succeeding. These types of clients are a large part of my practice. No matter what the topic is, when talking to these clients, that topic is a mess. Their lives sound like a country song in which their truck blew up, the dog ran away, and the wife had an affair.

I am always amazed how many different things are in a constant state of chaos in my clients' lives. Everything that could be going wrong is going wrong. I have had clients who in one week were fired, had their house broken into, had Child Protective Services investigate them, dealt with a divorce, and something else terrible that I cannot remember.

Most, if not all, of the problems in their lives are results of their actions. Obviously, no clients want to hear that they need to get their lives together and stop having so many problems. You can think it, but I would not recommend saying it. Good defense lawyers must remember that they are defense lawyers and not social workers. With these types of clients, it is easy to get sucked into their drama. If a client hires me for a DUI case, I have to be careful not to get sucked into their divorce case.

Con Artists/Manipulative Clients

These clients are almost always a subset of the frequent flier clients already discussed. It is very rare that a client who is a con artist or a manipulator is a first timer. Sometimes, you will be able to tell right away that they are trying to scheme something or trick you into something. Other times, it will not be as obvious. This can still be dangerous. The main thing I can teach you about these clients is to stay away from them. No amount of money is worth the headaches from these clients.

Usually, these clients will have some plan or scheme that they will try to involve you in. Other times, they will have elaborate stories as to why they will pay you later. I have heard stories about everything from income tax returns, to inheritances, to medical settlements. Sometimes, they think the lawyer is just plain dumb. I once had a client charged with check fraud try to pay me with a personal check.

The Constitutionalists

Every lawyer who has been practicing long enough has run across a constitutionalist. A constitutionalist is a person who has a "unique" interpretation of the constitution. And by unique, I mean a definition that is different from that of people trained in the law. Many constitutionalists enjoy doing legal research and want to share their finding with anyone who will listen. Their research is wrong most of the time, but this does not discourage them.

Constitutionalists vary from person to person, but many of them hold the following beliefs:

1. The income tax is unconstitutional and they do not have to pay it.
2. Courts do not have jurisdiction over them for various reasons.
3. Lawyers do not know what they are doing and do not give proper advice.
4. Judges do not have the right to impose penalties.
5. Signing paperwork given to them by the court is unconstitutional and they do not have to sign the paperwork.
6. They can bring their friends with them to court to speak on their behalf, even though their friends are not licensed lawyers.

I have been fortunate that I have not run across too many constitutionalists but the few I have dealt with have been memorable. Several years ago, I was representing a defendant who was charged with armed robbery. When I met with the defendant, he told me that the court did not have jurisdiction to hear his case because of a treaty he had researched.

He had found a treaty between Spain and the Colonies of the United States. The treaty dealt with ship embargos and trade between the two countries. According to my client, this treaty, from several hundred years ago, and dealing with ship trading, meant he could not be prosecuted.

When he brought this argument to the judge, the judge was very nice about hearing him out. The judge politely explained to the defendant that since he was not a ship, he did not think the treaty applied to his particular case. If only my client had been a ship, he might have gotten out of his armed robbery case.

Another client who I was representing on a criminal matter told me that the court had to dismiss his case because of the UCC. The UCC is the Uniform Commercial Code and deals with how businesses transact with each other. The UCC comes up when one company places an order with another company and then wants to return whatever it purchased. The UCC has absolutely nothing to do with criminal law, and, in fact, could not be farther away from the criminal justice system.

No matter how much I tried to reason with my client and tried to explain to him that the UCC did not apply to him for a number of reasons, he would not listen. He kept telling me that he had done his own research (which is never a good idea), and he knew that I was lying to him, and that the UCC finding meant that his case had to be dismissed. He was effectively his own pro se lawyer.

Pro se and constitutionalists also enjoy filing their own motions. The motions are generally a result of a creative Google search and contain little-to-no relevant law.

Sometimes, the law itself is relevant, but just not to the issue. There might be good law for a construction defect lawsuit but not for a disorderly conduct charge.

They often have a "legally trained friend" will write the motion for the defendant. Sometimes you can tell that someone else wrote the motion from looking at the wording. Usually, the defendant believes that if he or she puts in some kind of magical language, the case will automatically be dismissed. I can assure you, this will not work.

I recently saw a motion filed in one of the city courts where the defendant crossed out the name of the court and put in "Municipal Court of Terrorism." The motion also cited Arizona as a bankrupt legal fiction and an alter ego of the International Monetary Fund. The motion also claimed that Arizona had an alter ego, which was part of the International Monetary Fund. None of it had anything to do with the actual charges the defendant was facing.

A favorite pastime of some constitutionalists is suing prosecutors. Prosecutors are generally immune from prosecution, but this does not deter constitutionalists. Constitutionalist defendants will often sue prosecutors since the prosecutors are prosecuting a case against them and for no other reason.

I currently have a friend who is being sued by a constitutionalist. My friend works part time as a prosecutor and she was not happy with this. The lawsuits have been dismissed several times, but the former defendant keeps refilling them. This former defendant is convinced that she knows the law better than the courts and nothing anyone tells her will change her mind.

Another common characteristic of constitutionalists is that they will bring their friends with them as "counsel." These people have convinced themselves that if they go to court with their like-minded friends, the judge will see the law their way. Several years ago, I was appointed as an advisory lawyer on a case where a constitutionalist wanted to represent herself. The woman had been charged with driving on a suspended license, and she wanted to fight the license because according to her the federal government was an unconstitutional government; therefore, she could not be forced to have a driver's license. At the time of trial, she brought five people with her. One of the people was dressed like an old-time prospector. The guy proceeded to walk into the courtroom and sit with the woman at the defense table. The judge asked the gentleman if he was a lawyer. He told her he did not need to answer her question. She told him that she was asking because only lawyers can sit at the lawyer's table. This led into a long explanation by the gentleman how this is unconstitutional and that a law license is not required. Things went downhill from there as the gentleman took out his turn of the century typewriter, an antiquated device rarely seen in a courtroom nowadays.

Many constitutionalists believe that one does not need a license to practice law. I had a relative of a defendant come to court once and start asking me a bunch of questions about how I was handling their relative's case. The person had an attitude, so I asked him if he was a lawyer. He told me it was not relevant, and I told him it was since he was asking me questions about trial strategy. He further explained that anyone should be able to practice the law without the American Bar Association telling him or her if he or she can. I told him that I did not have time for his creative theories and walked away.

Undocumented Immigrants

Several years ago, the US Supreme Court came down with a decision called *Pedilla*.[1] The case involved an undocumented immigrant who had been convicted of a drug crime. As a result of the drug crime conviction, the defendant was deported.

The defendant appealed the decision saying that his defense lawyer did not warn him of the immigration consequences. The State argued that it is not the job of a defense lawyer to explain immigration consequences. Defense lawyers were also worried about the decision as it would affect how they would have to practice. The Supreme Court ruled that defense lawyers DID have to explain possible immigration consequences to their clients.

The decision was important because it effectively made defense lawyers become familiar with immigration law.

---

1. *Padilla v. Commonwealth of Kentucky*, 559 U.S. 356.

Before the decision, a defense lawyer could simply say, "I'm not an immigration lawyer, so I don't know the answer; go talk to an immigration lawyer." Depending on what part of the country you practice law in, this can be a big deal.

Arizona is home to a lot of immigrants. Many are from Mexico but they also come from Central and South America. Many are here as permanent immigrants, whereas others are here as seasonal workers. Immigration consequences can have a huge impact on the advice that defense lawyers give.

One example is diversion cases. Diversion cases can be different but they all work under the same basic principle. A person is allowed to take a class(es) and/or have probation, and if everything gets done, the criminal charge gets dismissed. Diversion is great for purposes of avoiding a criminal record. The problem is that when a person is going through immigration or applying for citizenship, many diversion dismissals are treated as convictions. I do not know why this is the case, but it is. What this means for me is that I have to know how the dismissal is treated in order to properly advise my client.

If my client has a shoplifting charge and she is eligible for diversion, I have to tell her that when she deals with immigration down the road, they will treat the class as a conviction impacting her decision now because of the consequences later. I talk to many defense lawyers who do not know this and end up hurting their clients.

Another aspect of representing undocumented defendants is dealing with deportation. In Maricopa County, when a person gets booked into the jail, his or her name is run through a federal database and the jail tries to establish if the person is undocumented. The system is far from perfect, and I have had more than one defendant who was either a legal resident or US citizen, yet the computer said he or she was an illegal resident.

If a suspect gets an immigration hold put on him or her, it means several bad things for the suspect. The first is that once the criminal case is over, the suspect will be sent to immigration jail. Once the suspect is in jail, he or she can try getting an immigration bond or be deported. Some defendants sign for voluntary deportation, whereas others choose to fight the deportation.

In our current 2017 political climate, there is an ever-increasing effort to find and deport undocumented immigrants. Only time will tell if this will change in the next several years.

The immigration holds are also a huge issue when someone has to surrender to the jail. Many jurisdictions will allow defendants to surrender themselves after they are convicted. The court will say, "Okay, you are convicted, but you can pick a self-surrender date and just show up to the jail to serve your sentence." However, if an undocumented resident surrenders, the jail will take the individual in, but it will not let the person out. Defense lawyers have to know this to properly advise their clients.

Imagine how shocked and horrified a client would be if he or she did not know about the immigration holds and ended up getting held and/or sent to immigration jail. An individual may think he or she is going to be there for only one or two days and end up in immigration custody for several months.

I remember one heartbreaking immigration case with a young woman. I was working in jail court as described in the prior chapter and one of the correctional officers informed me that the defendant I was talking to had an immigration hold on her. She had been arrested for driving on a suspended license. I told her she had an immigration hold, and she fell apart crying because she knew what it meant.

She told me she was in the United States on a student visa, but all her paperwork was at home. I called her family and asked them to bring the paperwork to the jail. I told the family that they needed to hurry because if they did not show up in time, the girl could be given over to immigration police custody. The family came down with the paperwork, but the jail supervisor was not convinced. It took the better part of the day, but we were finally able to convince the jail to drop the immigration hold, and the girl did not have to be handed over to immigration.

One other aspect of being a criminal defense lawyer in Arizona is dealing with human smuggling cases. Many people in Arizona have family in Central or South America and want to bring their family to the United States. Oftentimes, the American family member will pay a professional smuggler, often called a "coyote," to bring over his or her loved one(s).

Often, a large amount of money is involved, and the families may have to save up for months or even years to come up with the amount. Unfortunately for the families, the "coyotes" do not always keep their word. There are many cases where the "coyotes" change the price at the last minute. If the family or individual cannot pay the amount, one of two things will happen to the individual being transported. Either the individual will be held prisoner until the money is available, or the individual will be put to work. Often, the females who are held are forced into prostitution.

The people who are transported are often held in horrible conditions. They are usually held in what are known as "drop houses," and the "coyotes" have these "drop houses" throughout the city. When the houses are raided by the police, there can be anywhere from fifteen to thirty people held in one small space.

The Gamblers

"You gotta know when to hold 'em, Know when to fold 'em."

—*Kenny Rogers*

Clients will sometimes gamble in one of two ways. First, they will gamble in the hopes that they will not get caught and that they will get away with their crimes. Second, when they are caught, they believe that they can win at trial. I have represented many defendants who have held these beliefs. More often than not, they turn out to be wrong.

One of the most memorable gamblers of my career was a client in a case I assisted with when I was a new lawyer. I was helping a defense lawyer friend of mine on a case as a learning tool. My friend was a representing a drug dealer who was about to take a huge gamble. The drug dealer was incredibly successful and had not been arrested almost twenty years. One of the detectives working the case described him as one of the biggest pharmaceutical pill drug dealers in the Phoenix area.

The guy had been caught for a silly reason. He and his wife had an argument, and the police were called. When the police arrived, the argument was over, and as the police were about to leave, they noticed the defendant's car. What they noticed was that it was a type of flashy and expensive car that belonged in a rap video and not in the poor part of town. The police asked the guy about the car, and that was the beginning of the end.

The drug dealer did not have a good explanation, and his story changed from working in a family business to having good investments, and so on. The police started an investigation and soon discovered the extent of his drug operation. When they arrested him and raided his storage places, they found not only hundreds of thousands of dollars in pills and other drugs, but also hundreds of thousands of dollars in cash.

The good thing for the dealer was that he did not have any prior felony convictions. What hurt him was the extent of the drug operation he was running. The prosecutor made him a plea of somewhere between ten and fifteen years. The guy had hired a very expensive private lawyer who gave him terrible legal advice. When the client could no longer afford the private defense lawyer, the court appointed my friend as the drug dealer's defense attorney.

The client told my friend the legal advice he was given, and my friend immediately told him it was bad advice. The advice had to do with a Fourth Amendment issue and a first-year law student would know that the advice given by the first lawyer was wrong. The client thought the first lawyer was right since he was very expensive, and he thought my friend was wrong because he was court appointed.

The client turned down the plea and chose to proceed to trial. My friend advised the client that going to trial was a big gamble because if he was convicted, it would be possible for him to spend the rest of his life in jail. The client ignored this advice, and you can probably guess what happened after the trial. The client was sentenced to life in prison and is still in prison as I write this book.

I also had a client who took a big gamble. I was appointed on an assault case where my defendant was charged with punching a young man. According to the police reports, a family was walking around after a baseball game when my client came up to the mother, picked her up, and started swinging her around. The woman's sons asked him what he was doing, words were exchanged, and eventually a fight broke out.

According to my client, the woman asked him to pick her up and talked to him about how she liked his long hair. According to the mother, none of this occurred, and she had no idea why my client picked her up. As a side note, when my client was arrested, a large quantity of cash and drugs were found on him.

The prosecutor had made us a reasonable plea offer, and I told my client it was up to him if he wanted to take it, but in my opinion, he should take the deal since the prosecutor had a very strong case against him. The prosecutor not only had the entire family who would testify, but also onlookers who had witnessed the whole thing and would testify that my client had initiated the whole encounter.

My client was convinced that the judge would believe him over the family and not find him guilty. At the trial, it was clear that the witnesses were a lot more credible than my client. My client did bring a witness who wanted to testify to the fact that if my client "wanted to fuck some people up, he would have, and since the victims did not have serious injuries, it was clear that my client never hit them." Unfortunately, my client insisted on testifying, despite my best attempts to convince him otherwise. As all defense lawyers know, clients get to make two main decisions during their case. One is if they want to accept a plea agreement, the other is if they want to testify. The judge found my client guilty and gave him about twice as much jail as he would have received if he had taken the plea.

Betting on witnesses not showing up is another place where some defendants gamble with their own fate. Often, the prosecutor's case depends on a witness showing up or not showing up. Often, the police respond to the incident in question and by the time they respond there is nothing to see. Defendants often know, or are told by counsel, that their case hinges on a victim or witness showing up to testify against them.

Some defendants will send their case to trial knowing that the only chance they have of beating the charge is if the victim or witness does not show up. Good defense lawyers will always be clear with their clients that they cannot tell the victim or witnesses not to show up. There is a name for when defendants do this and it is called witness tampering. It is never good when you get a recording of your client calling the victim from the jail and telling him or her not to show up, or, better yet, threatening him or her into not showing up.

Sometimes, the gamble pays off and other times it does not. I have had so many cases where the client assured me that the victim was not showing up only to have the victim show up at the last second.

In misdemeanor cases, this is usually not a huge deal since the maximum sentence is a few months in jail. When dealing with felonies, the difference between a conviction and no conviction can be decades, or even life in prison.

Entitled Clients

I recently represented a young woman who was in her early twenties and was facing her third DUI. The police saw her sideswipe a parked car and began to follow her. When the police stopped her and asked if she knew why they were stopping her, she said, "No." The police asked her if she noticed that her rear view mirror was broken off, or if she noticed that she sideswiped a parked car, and she said that she did not.

The police recorded the entire conversation, and it was clear from watching the video that she was incredibly spoiled and entitled. When it came time for her to work out her jail arrangements, she asked me one particular request. (I thought she was joking at first, but she was not.) She asked me if the jail would allow her to bring in her purse dog because she liked carrying the dog with her.

I told her there was a zero percent chance that the jail would allow her to bring her dog with her. She seemed actually surprised by this and told me she thought it was unfair.

Entitled clients might be the most difficult group of clients to work with. Many of my entitled clients will say some variation of the following to me:

1. "I can't go to jail; I have a very busy schedule."
2. "Jail is for criminals, and I am not a criminal."
3. "I told the police that I donate a lot of money to their fundraisers, but he still had the audacity to arrest me."

4. "I'm worried what the accommodations will be like in jail."
5. "What if the jail has bad food?"
6. "Don't the police have anything better to do than to pull me over for stupid traffic violations?"
7. "The officer only pulled me over because he wanted to flirt with me."

Many of these clients feel like they are too important to be in trouble. Oftentimes, these clients think that the best course of action is to threaten the person pulling them over.

The following is very close to a word-for-word police report I had:

Officer: "Hello ma'am, do you know why I pulled you over?"

Defendant: "Because you have nothing better to do?"

Officer: "No, ma'am, it was because you committed six different traffic violations, and now that I am speaking to you I can smell an odor of an alcoholic beverage."

Defendant: "That's ridiculous. I'm a good driver and I don't need to answer your questions about if I have been drinking."

Officer: "Well, ma'am, you actually do. Please step out of the car; I want to make sure you are ok to drive."

Defendant: "You will be out of a job by the time I am done with you."

Everything is relative, so sometimes a client who is facing one day in jail will be more freaked out than another defendant about to spend twenty years in prison. If a person has never been in trouble and has an attitude that he or she is too important or rich to spend a day in jail, the individual will make sure that his or her lawyer is aware of this belief.

I have had many lawyers tell me that a client charged with a misdemeanor can be a lot more difficult to deal with than someone charged with a felony. This seems very counterintuitive but is sometimes true.

Another favorite move of entitled clients is to bring family along when meeting with their defense lawyer. I have had a defendant bring a spouse or parents. It is their job to tell me how special their family member is and that jail and other consequences of the crime are for other people and not for their family member. As I have said before, sometimes people have a hard time accepting responsibility for their actions.

Poor and Homeless Clients

"It is better to be rich and healthy than poor and sick."

—Russian proverb

I once represented a homeless man who was arrested for trespassing. His "trespassing" consisted of standing outside a homeless shelter and waiting for it to open. He was not being noisy or disruptive. My defendant was just standing there. He was waiting to get some food because he was hungry. The police said the homeless shelter was not open, even though he knew it would be soon, so he cited the homeless person. Would that same officer cite a business-person in a suit for trespassing for standing outside a bank and waiting for it to open?

The sad reality is that poor defendants are worse off in our system than people with money. There is no way around this fact. There are many examples of this, but one of the clearest has to do with jail costs.

Many people are surprised that they have to pay to go to jail. Although I do not know if this is the case in every state, I do know that in most of Phoenix area, defendants have to pay for their own jail costs. The reason for this is that almost none of the cities own their own jails. The cities send their defendants to the county jail, and the county jail bills the cities for each defendant.

As cities continue to struggle with their own budgets, they have started to pass along the jail costs to the defen-dant. In theory, there is nothing wrong with making some-one pay for their own jail bill. Judges are fond of saying, "Someone has to pay for the jail, and it's not fair to make the taxpayers pay for someone else's sentence."

This seems odd to me. My taxes pay for schools— even though I do not have kids. My taxes pay for the fire department—even if my house is not on fire. We as a society have agreed that we will all chip in to pay for things so everything keeps working. It seems reasonable to me that if a defendant is poor and not able to pay for his or her jail time, the cost would be waived. Some judges will reduce or waive jail costs, but many will not under any circumstances.

The problem is that many defendants cannot afford the jail costs. First, the jail costs are not cheap. The rates are always changing, but as of this writing, the county charges about two hundred dollars for the first day, and about one hundred dollars for each subsequent day. Compounding the problem, some cities have established a vicious cycle of incarceration and jail costs.

Some cities will arrest defendants for not paying their own jail costs. So, for example, a defendant is ordered to pay a thousand dollars in jail costs. The defendant never pays the jail costs because either he or she is not able to or does not want to. The city issues a warrant for that defendant, and he or she ends up back in jail. Now, the city is charged more in jail costs from the county, and the city is out more money than they would have been in the first place.

Often, when I represent people who are in custody, they tell me that they wanted to pay their jail costs but were simply not able to. Many of my court-appointed defendants make a few hundred bucks a week if they are lucky. When someone who makes a few hundred bucks a week is told to pay several thousand dollars in jail costs, it becomes clear that the chances of the jail costs being paid are very small.

If a defendant has money, he or she simply pays the jail costs and moves on with his or her life. If a defendant is poor, like many of mine are, he or she falls into a vicious cycle of being in and out of jail for the jail costs. I have represented defendants who have been in and out of jail because of jail costs for years.

Another problem with arresting people for not paying their own jail costs is that defendants often end up losing their jobs because they are in jail. Many of my defendants have jobs that they will lose for simply missing a day or two. Not only is the city running up a higher jail cost tab, but it is keeping people from going to work and providing for their families.

One of my cases that showed the glaring problem with jail costs involved a homeless defendant. The defendant had been charged with sleeping in the park—not yelling in the park, not masturbating in the park, but simply sleeping there because he had nowhere else to go. The prosecutor wanted to lock him up for six months because he had prior convictions.

All of his prior convictions were from crimes related to being homeless, like dumpster diving, public intoxication, and trespassing. No matter how much I argued with the prosecutor that it was insane to lock up a human being in jail for half a year for sleeping in a park, she would not budge. Adding insult to injury, the prosecutor also wanted my defendant to pay a thousand-dollar fine.

We ended up pleading to the judge and letting the judge decide the sentence. The judge was unreasonable and gave my defendant six months in jail. The judge, like the prosecutor, pointed out that my defendant had many prior convictions. So now, not only is my defendant in jail for six months, but he is also assessed close to twenty thousand dollars in jail costs. Obviously, he will never pay the huge amount, as he is homeless, so the city will have to pay. Imagine the kind of housing, work training, and alcohol treatment that could be bought for twenty thousand dollars.

Another one of my cases was similar as the city could have chosen to save itself a lot of money but chose not to. My defendant was another homeless man, and he was charged with disorderly conduct. His crime was yelling and pointing a stick at a park ranger.

The client had been arrested and kept refusing transport, so he kept missing his in-custody court dates. I went to the jail to meet with the client, and it was clear that he had mental health problems. By the time I had seen him in jail, he had been in custody for close to a month, and the city already owed thousands of dollars to the county for housing my defendant.

I went to the prosecutor and asked him to dismiss the case. I explained that my defendant had already been in custody for a month; he would keep refusing to be transported for his court dates; and the city would keep racking up thousands of dollars in jail costs. The prosecutor refused to dismiss the case because the park ranger, who was the victim in the case, did not want the case dismissed. My defendant ended up serving almost six months in jail, and the city got another jail bill for almost twenty thousand dollars.

Another place where the poor are worse off than people with money is when it comes to court costs. When you are convicted of a crime, whether it is a misdemeanor or felony, there are many little costs and fines that are added by court. One of the mandatory fines for a DUI conviction is a prison construction fine, which is fairly ironic for several reasons. Although both poor and wealthy defendants have to pay these fines, the ability to pay them is drastically different. Often, the fines are several hundred dollars, which is no big deal to someone who can afford it. However, the fines are a huge deal to someone with little or no money.

Another problem for defendants with little or no money is the fee that the courts now charge to set up a payment plan. The fee is normally about twenty dollars, which does not sound like a lot until you realize that some of my defendants might only make forty or fifty dollars a day. A defendant with money does not have to pay this fee, as he or she does not need a payment plan.

A lot of the time with poor or homeless defendants, the crime they are realistically being charged with is being poor. Many cities now have ordinances that prohibit panhandling and the police can arrest people for having signs asking for money. Although I understand that cities do not want people panhandling on every corner, arresting these people often just makes things worse.

My most memorable panhandling case was several years ago and involved a dad and his daughter. The dad was an immigrant from Eastern Europe and could not find work. Part of the reason he could not find work was that he did not have a work permit and was not a US citizen. He was also a single parent to his small daughter, and they had no family or support system.

The dad resorted to panhandling as it was the only way he thought he could make money. The police arrested him not only for panhandling but also for child endangerment, claiming that he was endangering his daughter. I talked to the prosecutor and told them that the daughter was not in any danger, as she was simply standing with her dad on the sidewalk. The dad was holding her with one hand and holding a sign asking for donations with his other hand.

Initially, the prosecutor wanted him to serve thirty days in jail. The prosecutor did not care that the daughter would have to be taken to a foster home and ripped apart from the only family she had. The prosecutor also wanted my client to do expensive and long parenting classes. I tried explaining the prosecutor that my client not only did not need the classes but could not afford them as well.

Poor defendants not being able to pay for classes is another huge issue. Although ordering someone with an alcohol problem to take alcohol abuse classes sounds like a good idea, the problem arises when those defendants are not able to pay for the classes they have been ordered to take. Many prosecutors will set up plea agreements where there is suspended jail time upon classes or a program. What this means is that there is additional jail time that the defendant only has to serve if he or she does not complete the class or program.

The problem with the classes is that they are very expensive for poor people. A typical class will run from anywhere from ten to fifty-two weeks and cost about twenty dollars per class. As discussed, this is a lot of money for many defendants. If a defendant has money, he or she simply does the class and moves on with his or her life. If a defendant is poor and cannot take the classes, he or she will end up serving more time in jail and owing more jail costs.

I have had countless defendants tell me that they want to do the class or the program and think it would help them, but they simply cannot afford it. I have even had defendants ask for classes when the prosecutor was not asking for them, as the defendants knew they needed help for their addiction or problem. Not only do defendants have to pay for their own classes, they are always being charged additional fees for not being able to pay.

In a typical case, a defendant will start going to the classes, and, at some point, will not be able to afford them anymore. The class provider will report the defendant as non-complaint to the court. To the provider, there is no distinction if someone stops going to the classes because they do not want to go, or if someone simply cannot afford to go.

Many poor defendants not only have the hurdle of paying for the classes but even getting to the classes. If a defendant has money, he or she simply drives to the classes. Many of my defendants cannot afford cars, and yet others have had their licenses suspended for years and are not able to drive.

Once reported as noncomplaint, the defendant has to come back to court and ask to be let back into the class, but there is an additional fee that the class provider charges for someone to get back into the class. As you can see, many defendants fall into a vicious cycle of jail, fines, and classes.

Another problem with the classes is that they cause defendants to miss work. Some of the classes have evening and weekend programs, but others do not. Sometimes, defendants have to make the following choice: They can go to the class, avoid further jail time, and risk losing their jobs, or they can go to work, get kicked out of the classes, and fall into a further hole with court.

The final and maybe largest hurdle that low-income defendants face is the quality of legal services they can afford. Public defenders do amazing work, but they are all overworked. Ask any public defender and they will tell you that they do not have enough time to spend with each client. Public defenders have incredible amounts of knowledge and experience, but most simply do not have enough time.

The defense lawyers who have more time to devote to each client are private lawyers. Having more time to spend with each defendant gives the defendant several huge advantages. First, it gives the lawyer time to fully investigate the case. Second, the lawyer can better prepare the client for trial.

I have a friend who is one of the three best DUI lawyers in Arizona. He also charges a lot of money for his services. When my friend has a client with an upcoming trial, he will spend close to three days prepping that client for trial. He will do mock direct and cross-examinations and do anything he needs to do make the client ready to testify. Having this kind of time is simply an unrealistic dream for most public defenders. The problem is not the public defenders, but the states and counties that refuse to properly fund the public defender's offices. It is hard for politicians to win elections on promises of funding public defender's offices. Most voters just want to hear how tough on crime politicians are.

A related issue to the type of lawyers poor clients can afford is the type of experts those same defendants can afford. As we will get into later, experts can make a huge impact on a criminal trial. A good expert can make or break a case. The problem for poor defendants is that the good experts are expensive. Simple supply and demand tells us that a sought-after expert will charge more. Some public defender's offices have their own experts on retainer, and some of these experts are excellent. Unfortunately, many public defender's offices not only lack experts on retainer but simply cannot afford any experts.

There is case law stating that poor defendants can have experts appointed for them at little or no cost, but courts are often reluctant to appoint the experts. A good expert can cost many thousands of dollars, and the truth of the matter is that courts have to watch what they spend. I have had judges deny my requests for experts, telling me that I do not really need the experts. You do not have to be a law school graduate to know that when a judge is telling a lawyer what they do or do not need, there is a problem.

Chapter Four

Crimes

Felony versus Misdemeanor Crimes

All criminal offenses are broken down into two classifications: felony offenses and misdemeanor offenses. Felony offenses are those that can be punished by over one year of incarceration. Misdemeanor offenses are everything else. Another way to look at the two is that felony offenses are more serious in nature. There are several important differences between the two types of cases.

One difference is how much a defense lawyer can charge for the work. Defense lawyers will charge more for felonies than misdemeanors. This is because the stakes are higher, trials take longer, and, in general, felony cases take more time than misdemeanor cases. A misdemeanor trial will usually take anywhere from several hours to several days. A felony trial will usually last from several days to several months.

Although felony defense lawyers charge more per case, this does not necessarily mean they make more overall. If you take one felony case and charge ten thousand dollars; it takes all your time for one month and you cannot take any more cases, but another lawyer takes five misdemeanor cases at three thousand dollars each in that same month. In this example, the misdemeanor lawyer has made more money.

After practicing for several years, most defense lawyers find themselves focusing on one type of case. There are some lawyers who split their time between felony cases and misdemeanor cases but they are the exception. Most lawyers end up doing primarily felony or misdemeanor work. I think part of the reason for this is that if you do mostly felony work, you get mostly felony referrals and vice versa. Also, there is so much to learn in criminal defense that it is hard to be really good at misdemeanor and felony work at the same time, so many lawyers choose to focus on one or the other.

Some defense lawyers make a conscious effort to go into one type of case work over another. Some lawyers do not want to do felony work because they do not want to be stuck in trial. Some lawyers chose to do more felony work because they do not like misdemeanor work. I know several lawyers who do not like felony work because they will not represent sex offenders and those cases tend to come up a lot. Although some lawyers make an active choice to do one type of case over another, many more fall into one over the other by chance.

Currently, I do more misdemeanor work than felony work, but this was not by design. I get more calls and referrals for misdemeanors, so I end up doing more of that type of work. If I started getting more felony cases, I would do more felony work. When I was starting out, I did not make a conscious choice to do one type of work over the other. In my experience, this is what happens to most defense lawyers.

Driving under the Influence (DUI)

DUI law is an ever-evolving and complicated area of criminal defense. There are two reasons for the fluidity of DUI cases. First, The DUI laws themselves are always changing. States are always changing what the DUI limits are. Now there is an entire area of DUI defense that is focused on drug DUI cases. As more and more states legalize marijuana, yet a new area of DUI defense has emerged. Second, just as the DUI laws keeps changing and evolving, so do the methods that defense lawyers use to defend DUI cases. DUI defense lawyers must not only be proficient in trial but must also know all the scientific aspects of defending DUI cases.

Another aspect of DUI defense work that makes it especially difficult is that oftentimes the main witness for the prosecution is the police officer who stopped the driver and usually the police officer witnesses the actual crime.

Defense lawyers must understand this and be prepared for the trial. If your defendant is accused of shooting someone at a house party, chances are high that all the witnesses will be civilians who are not used to testifying. A police officer is a trained witness who generally receives training on how to testify. This makes the work of a defense lawyer more complicated.

I once represented a defendant who was charged with a DUI in a stolen street sweeper. Not only had my defendant stolen a street sweeper, but he had also run over the guy he stole it from. The street sweeper vehicle had been parked as the worker went inside a local business. My client jumped onto the machine, somehow got it started, and began driving away. The street sweeper driver noticed this and ran out to yell at my defendant to give him his street sweeper back. My client kept driving the street sweeper and ran the poor guy over. Luckily, he was not seriously hurt. The story illustrates why we have DUI laws. People do not make good decisions while impaired. I guess it is possible that my client would have stolen the street sweeper sober, but I doubt it.

It is not a secret that alcohol affects people's ability to make sound decisions. This is part of the reason we have DUI laws. One of the clearest examples I ever had on this was when I was representing a young woman charged with a DUI.

There was nothing special about the case, except that she called the police on herself. Dispatchers got a call of a drunk driver, and the caller asked that the police be sent to check on the drunk driver. When the police showed up, the young woman was parked in the middle of the street still on the phone with the 911 dispatcher. The officer took the phone from the woman and told the dispatcher that he was on scene.

The woman's night went downhill from there, as she got naked in the back of the police car and peed all over herself and the back seat. Needless to say, this was probably the most embarrassing incident of the young woman's life. When I spoke to the woman in court, she was mortified as she did not remember any of this. All she remembered was being at a party and drinking with her friends, and the next thing she is at the police station with all her clothes missing. I doubt that this young woman will ever get another DUI, as I think she learned from her mistake. Not everyone learns from his or her mistakes. Oftentimes, I realize that when my client gets a DUI, it is the worst day of his or her life. Most of my DUI clients are not career criminals and have never been arrested before. Being taken to the police station to be processed for a DUI is incredibly stressful and a good defense lawyer must be cognizant of what their client is going through, not only during the arrest but also throughout the entire criminal process.

I recently represented a young man who was charged with a DUI while driving himself back to jail. He was doing a work release program where the jail released him during the day to go to work. Then, he had to turn himself back in at night. On the way to jail, he crashed his car into a gas station. When the police tested his blood, he had an incredibly high amount of morphine and codeine in his system. When I showed his blood results to my expert, the expert asked if the defendant was dead. He explained to me that such high levels of the drug usually resulted in overdose and death. Most people would not think it would be a good idea to get insanely high before turning oneself into jail, but my client thought otherwise.

One of the strangest DUI cases I ever dealt with involved an African American gentleman who said he had been charged with a DUI because the police were racially profiling him. What was strange about his case was that he had never been pulled over. The police officer noticed him only as my defendant ran his car into the officer's parked car. Imagine how surprised the officer was to see someone run into his parked car in a parking lot. It was soon established that my client was impaired, and he was cited for a DUI. I kept telling my client that he was the one who initiated the police contact, but my client would not listen and kept insisting that the case should be thrown out because the officer had racially profiled him. A case like this is an important lesson for defense lawyers as it is a reminder that some of your clients will never be reasonable. You can explain to them all day long that they were the ones who ran into the parked police car but they will not listen.

Defendants not wanting to take responsibility for their DUI charges are an all too common theme. Part of the reason people have a hard time taking responsibility for their charges is because they do not think of themselves as criminals. When I represent lifelong gang members, they do not mind thinking of themselves as criminals. When I represent people who have never been in trouble their whole lives and are now facing DUI charges, they have a hard time with it because it is new to them. Having a criminal conviction is understandably scary to people.

Sometimes, people do not want to take responsibility for their DUI charges because of how it makes them look. I represented a woman once who was charged with a DUI while she was pregnant. She told me she did not want to plead guilty because she knew how bad it looked for a pregnant woman to be convicted of a DUI.

Not all DUI clients are difficult. There are clients who walk into my office and tell me they want to take responsibility for their actions and they knew they were wrong. I often feel bad for my DUI clients.

One client was an immigrant from an extremely poor country who came to Arizona to work on a farm. He had been pulled over and his blood alcohol concentration (BAC) was .081, which means he was barely over the .08 legal limit. We had a trial, and I was able to get the state's criminalist (scientist) to admit that the difference between being over the limit and not was about an ounce of beer. What this means is that if my client had drunk one less ounce of alcohol, he would have been under the limit. There was also no testimony that the alcohol impaired my client. The jury deliberated for hours and returned with a hung verdict. This meant that the prosecutor could re-file the charges, and we would have to go through another trial. I tried to reason with the prosecutor to not re-file the charges, but he would not listen. We had a second trial and my client was convicted.

Defending DUI cases is difficult for several reasons. The first is that most police departments have specific officers who are assigned to special DUI task forces. What this means for defense lawyers is that you are dealing with officers who have an incredible amount of experience in handling DUI investigations. I often deal with officers who have conducted thousands of DUI investigations. Their experience means that they are less likely to make a mistake. As discussed, I like to think that police officers are careful because they know defense lawyers are watching over their shoulders.

One way of successfully challenging DUI cases is to show that there was a mistake with the blood—showing there is a mistake in how the blood was drawn, processed, or analyzed. If there is a mistake, most prosecutors will try fighting the defense lawyer by saying there is no mistake. Some prosecutors are more reasonable than others. There are supervising prosecutors in the Phoenix area who will never admit a problem no matter how damning the evidence.

Another method of challenging DUI charges is to try to show that there was no legal basis for the stop. An officer needs a valid reason to stop a driver. The reasons can be incredibly minor, but there still has to a reason. If a defense lawyer can show that there was no legal reason for the stop, the case could be thrown out. The officer is, of course, going to argue that there was a legal reason for the stop. The officer will never say, "Well, I didn't have a great reason for stopping your defendant, but he has brown skin, so I assumed he was guilty of something."

Several years ago, I represented a young man who was charged with a DUI. The police had responded to a "shots fired" call and the caller said that the shooter was Hispanic and had gotten into a white car. My client was Hispanic and had been driving a white car. When the police stopped my client, they realized that he was not the shooter they were looking for, but they did arrest my client for a DUI.

I argued that this was a bad stop since the description of the shooter was too broad and that the police could not stop every white car they saw. The area where this occurred was a predominantly Hispanic area, so when the police said that the driver matched the description, it was too broad. The judge did not accept my argument, and my client was eventually convicted of a DUI.

Drugs

"Ignore that nightmare in the bathroom. Just another ugly refugee from the Love Generation, some doom-struck gimp who couldn't handle the pressure. My lawyer has never been able to accept the notion—often espoused by reformed drug abusers and especially popular among those on probation—that you can get a

lot higher without drugs than with them. And neither have I, for that matter."

—*Hunter S. Thompson*

It would be impossible and foolish to write a book about the criminal defense world without talking about drugs. Sometimes, the drug stories are funny. I represented a woman charged with drug possession who called the police on her drug dealer. The woman told the police that her dealer had sold her a poor-quality methamphetamine and that she wanted her money back. The officer asked the woman if she had thought about the implications of calling the police to report a bad drug buy. The woman told the officer that she had not.

Another time, I represented a woman who was outraged that an officer told her that he thought that she was a heroin addict. I asked her if she was a heroin addict, as I was trying to figure out why she got so mad at the officer. She told me that she was actually a crack addict and that she thinks heroin is disguising and would never touch it. More often than not, the stories are more tragic than funny.

Many drug cases involve kids in one way or another. I have represented many defendants who were living in messy houses with small kids; some of them were so messy that you would think they could be features on a TV show about hoarders. I have seen pictures and police reports that were so disgusting, they were hard to think about. Generally, Child Protective Services (CPS) takes the kids away. I have spoken with defendants who have called CPS, asking to have their kids taken away from them since they knew they were unfit to take care of them. It is hard to imagine that some kids are in such a bad situation that they are better-off without their own parents.

There are several things to keep in mind when dealing with clients who have drug issues. The first is that many clients with substance issues want help in getting sober. I would say most of my clients with drug issues have told me that they want to get help for their addiction. Secondly, remember that you are not a substance abuse counselor, doctor, or social worker. Your job as a defense lawyer is to help clients with their criminal case. If you can get them into treatment as a way of resolving the case, or as a means of making the prosecutor happy, that is great.

My point is that it is not your job to treat your clients for their substance abuse problem. Not only is it what you are there for, but unless you have a background in this kind of work, you are not qualified for it. Not trying to treat the client yourself does not mean that you do not care about your client's substance abuse issue or that you are not empathetic to it. Understand what you are able to do and what you should not try to do.

Thirdly, remember that while clients lying to their defense lawyers is nothing new, the highest number of my clients who do lie to me have a drug problem. It is beyond the scope of this book to explain this, but the important part for you as the defense lawyer is to know that if your clients have a drug problem, they may be lying to you.

Lastly, many of your clients who have drug issues were initially given some kind of drug by a doctor, often after some kind of injury. About a year ago, I represented a young girl who had a sports injury dating back to her college years. After surgery for the injury, her doctor gave her a very powerful drug for her pain. She took the medication as prescribed but felt terrible when she tried to go off the medication. She took the prescription for months, and when it ran out, she could not function without the drug. Over the next several months, she turned to street drugs to get the same feeling and relief that she had from the prescription.

When I was assigned to her case, she was addicted to every drug she could obtain, had lost her job, and had started stealing to pay for her habit. When I represented her, she had warrants in three different cities.

There used to be a time when some people said that they were a drug addict, it was automatically assumed that they were addicted to illegal street drugs such as heroin or meth. Today, more and more people are addicted to legal drugs that they once had prescriptions for.

Society still looks at street drugs and prescription drugs differently, even though they are two sides of the same coin. Both forms of drugs can ruin people's lives and are incredibly easy to get addicted to. It does not matter if someone is addicted to a street drug or a prescription drug; he or she will go to great lengths to get more of that drug.

Many people do not understand how powerful many of the prescription medications are. I have had drug addicts tell me that they have taken pills that are more powerful than any dose of heroin or any other street drug. As science keeps making advances in pharmacology, the medications will keep getting stronger and stronger. Even worse, the symptoms people experience when they try to go off the various medications are horrible. People experience everything from not being able to sleep, to throwing up, to not being able to function at work, school, or in their home life.

Prescription addiction is not only hitting poor people. There are also a good number of professionals who get in trouble with pain pills and end up getting charged with buying the pills illegally or with driving under the influence of the drugs. The problem goes beyond medications given for pain relief.

There are also a number of sleeping pills on the market that get people into a lot of legal trouble. I have had cases where defendants took a sleeping medication and went driving while asleep. Can you imagine how scary that is? The person driving in the vehicle next to you might not be aware that he or she is driving. I have had experts tell me that not only there are reported cases of people driving on sleeping pills and not knowing it, but also there are reported cases of people having sex and not knowing it. The sleeping pills are especially dangerous when mixed with alcohol and can even be fatal.

Today, many of my defendants use street drugs and prescription drugs. Often, the street drugs are easier to get, but they will use whatever they can get their hands on. Oftentimes, when I talk to my clients and ask what they are addicted to, they will tell me, "Everything."

Unfortunately, I think the prescription medication problem will only continue to get worse. Not only will pills keep getting stronger, but also the American population will continue to age, which means more and more people will be taking powerful pain relief medications.

One of the places where our criminal justice system could improve the most is in how we deal with nonviolent drug crimes. This is by no means a new idea but one worth stressing. I have had countless defendants tell me that they want to go to rehab and they actually want the court to order rehab. These cries for help often fall on deaf ears, and the defendants are simply put in jail with no treatment. If someone has a drug problem, this person needs treatment and counseling. Simply putting him or her in jail does not change anything.

Some courts are trying to be better about offering treatment and classes, but many still take the old approach of just throwing people in jail. Some jails offer treatment programs, but many do not. Without treatment, the person has the same addiction when they come out of jail.

The notion of not offering classes does not make sense on a moral level, but it also does not make sense financially. In general, it costs a lot more money to lock someone up than to put that person in treatment. If a person gets treatment, then that person at least has the chance to change his or her life. If a person is simply put in jail, the chance of that person's life changing is almost nonexistent.

Not all police departments and prosecutors are the same on this issue. Some prosecutors are a lot more reasonable when it comes to punishing people charged with simple drug possession crimes. Other prosecutors try to come down on these individuals as hard as they can.

There is one prosecutor I always have had the same battle with. Our conversations go like this:

Me: "Why are you asking for six months jail and a thousand-dollar fine for my defendant? All they had on them was a pipe?"

Prosecutor: "They need to go to jail because they have priors."

Me: "He has priors because he is a drug addict and needs help."

Prosecutor: "I still want six months jail."

Me: "Will you reduce the fine? He is very poor and is sometimes homeless."

Prosecutor: "No, he can set up a payment plan with the court."

One of the best examples of how things could be done a lot better and fairer can be seen if we examine how marijuana crimes are prosecuted. In many states, including Arizona, it is still a felony to possess any amount of marijuana.

There is a diversion class for people charged with possession for the first time, but the class is long and costs thousands of dollars. If the person does not complete the class, the person becomes a convicted felon and, for all intents and purposes, the person's life is ruined. And why is it ruined? Because the person had a joint.

Another common injustice is when cops arrest people for not even having drugs, but having drug paraphernalia. I have represented defendants who were stopped with a pipe that had the smell of marijuana in it, and the prosecutor would try giving them months in jail.

Punishing drug generates a lot of revenue. It is big business not only for the federal agencies but also for local police departments. Local police departments know they can get easy arrests for simple drug crimes and then charge the defendants fines. I routinely see people charged with drug paraphernalia crimes where their fines range from a few hundred dollars to thousands. Now multiply the fines from one person times all the people arrested in a year for the same offense and you can see how punishing drug crimes is big business.

I am always amazed at the discrepancy in how our system distinguishes alcohol from marijuana. A person can have a keg of alcohol and no one cares. That same person can have one joint and will be arrested and charged with a felony. Today, as more and more states figure out the reality of what marijuana is and is not, hopefully things will begin to change. To further demonstrate how harshly our system punishes people who use or sell marijuana, all we need to do is look at the Arizona law dealing with the punishment of distribution of marijuana.

The following is taken directly from the Arizona Revised Statute Section §13-3405 and §13-702:

> As with possession for personal use, penalties depend on the amount of the marijuana involved.
>
> Possession of less than two pounds of marijuana for sale is a Class 4 felony, punishable by up to a sentence of one to four years.
>
> Possession of between two and four pounds of marijuana for sale is a Class 3 felony, punishable by a sentence of two to nine years.
>
> Possession of between four pounds or more of marijuana for sale is a Class 2 felony, punishable by a sentence of three to ten years.

Manslaughter is also a Class 2 Felony in Arizona. This means the legislature has decided that selling marijuana is just as bad as killing someone. Does this make sense? Arizona Courts put someone in prison for ten years for something that is perfectly legal next door in Colorado.

What makes all of this worse is that when someone has prior felony convictions, the punishments increase dramatically. The penalty for a second offense can be close to double than that for a first offense. The idea makes sense, as we want to punish people who keep getting in trouble. The problem with that is not on paper—but in reality.

Many low-income young people get into selling drugs because there are few other options for making money. What this means is that many of my defendants in their early twenties already have one or two prior convictions for selling drugs. Now, those same defendants are facing huge prison sentences for doing one of the only jobs that was available to them.

I know the conservative line here is that no one is forced to sell drugs and kids from horrible areas need to pull themselves up by their bootstraps. I would encourage those people to try living where some of my defendants live and see how successful they are at pulling themselves up by their bootstraps.

Prostitution

"Grown men should not be having sex with prostitutes unless they are married to them."

—*Jerry Falwell*

The above quote from the always-entertaining Mr. Falwell demonstrates this country's complex relationship with prostitution. Different prosecuting offices and police departments have placed different levels of importance of going after prostitution. In other words, some law enforcement agencies see it as more of a threat to public safety than others.

One of the best examples I ever saw of selective enforcement involved a DUI investigation. An officer pulled up to my defendant's car and recognized his passenger as a "well-known prostitute." The prostitute was performing a sex act on my defendant when the police walked up the car. As the prostitute saw the police, she jumped out of the car and started running away. The officer described the prostitute as extremely large and wearing very high heels. I bring this up because—if the officer wanted to catch the woman, he probably could have. The officer chose not to pursue the woman. As a defense lawyer, I see no shortage of prostitution cases.

In general, prostitutes are at a bigger disadvantage than escorts. One of the big differences between the two is that many prostitutes get their clients on the street. Soliciting clients on the street is worse for several reasons. The first reason is that it is easier for the police to notice you and arrest you. Oftentimes, it is clear when someone is soliciting a client on the street. Second, sex workers on the street are more susceptible to attack since they are out in the open. Not that escorts are not susceptible to attacks, but, in my experience, prostitutes are much more vulnerable.

Oftentimes, the prostitutes have a substance abuse issue and are on the street to feed their addictions. I have represented many prostitutes who were very honest with me about their drug habits and the only way to pay for their expensive drugs was to become a prostitute. Sometimes, the women are so bad off that they will accept being paid in other means besides cash.

Many prostitutes are abused and assaulted by their clients. I have represented more than one prostitute who came to court with one or two black eyes.

Most prostitutes have a pimp and will sometimes bring their pimps to court with them. The pimp will usually post bail because he needs the woman to be out earning money, which she cannot do if she is in custody. Usually when the pimp comes to court, he will not identify himself as a pimp. There have been some exceptions. I once represented a prostitute who brought her pimp to court, and he was dressed for the part. He wore an actual crown with jewels, a regal robe, and he had a cane.

When I meet pimps, they are always introduced to me an "uncle," a "concerned family friend," or as the "boyfriend" or "husband". It is usually easy to tell that these men are actually pimps because they always know a lot about the law. They always know more about the prostitution or escorting statute than someone should who is not in the industry. I have had "uncles" tell me that their "niece" was cited under the wrong subsection. Sometimes, the pimp actually is the husband. I had been a fairly young defense lawyer when I was assigned a prostitution case. When I met the defendant at the pretrial conference, she asked if her husband could sit in on the consultation. I agreed, and we started going over the police report. I had not read the police report prior to the court date because the prosecutor had just provided it to me.

The woman was busted in an undercover sting, and I was going to read the report. Before I read the undercover officers' report, I read the arresting officers' report, and this was when things got weird. After the woman was arrested, she told the officers that her husband was her pimp. Now I knew that the guy in the room with us was not only her husband but also her pimp.

Oftentimes, the prostitutes will have received bad legal advice, which is part of the reason they are seeing me. Someone started a popular rumor, stating that as long as the prostitute did not touch the money there cannot be an arrest for prostitution. This is wrong. All that is required is for money to be discussed in the context of it being exchanged for sexual services. There does not need to be any money displayed.

One prostitute I represented would not believe me. She had been arrested, along with her friend, for soliciting an undercover vice officer. The police not only had the officer's testimony but video AND audio of the entire sting as well. In the video, you could hear my defendant discuss prices and what those prices included.

My defendant kept telling me that she was innocent because she never took the money from the officer. We were all set for trial, but she decided to plead guilty at the last moment. This is why it is a good idea to ONLY take legal advice from your lawyer and not your "coworkers."

Domestic Violence Offenses

Every state is a little different, but in Arizona, a domestic violence (DV) offense occurs when the victim is a family member, cohabitant, or someone with whom you are in a sexual relationship. Since the definition under Arizona law includes anyone you are living with, a person can be charged with a DV offense against a roommate. As a defense lawyer, it is important that you understand the lifelong consequences your clients could be suffering if they are convicted of a DV offense.

If someone is applying for a job with an assault conviction, the employer does not know what happened but might assume it was a bar fight or a street altercation. When a person is applying for a job with a DV conviction, the employer will automatically assume the person with a conviction is a wife beater. Punching a stranger in a bar is no better or worse than punching your significant other, but there is a distinction between the two for most people.

Another implication of a DV offense in Arizona is that there are mandatory classes. The minimum number of classes is twenty-six, and there can be as many as fifty-two. Each class also costs about twenty dollars. Although DV prevention classes are a good idea, they are assigned automatically whether they are warranted or not. Another problem with the classes, as already discussed, is that many people cannot afford to follow through with them and end up back in court because of it.

The least expensive classes still come to about five hundred dollars, which is a fortune to many of my clients. The clients fall into a vicious cycle in which they cannot afford the classes and get in trouble for not being able to afford the classes, and it just keeps going and going.

Depending on what court you are in, there may also be jail involved if the charge is a misdemeanor. Generally, DV cases are misdemeanors, unless there is a long record of abuse, or if there is a serious injury or something else unique about the case. If the case is a felony, the defendant is facing prison, as is the case with all felonies. In one of the cities where I practice, thirty days in jail is the norm for a DV assault or DV.

I have had many DV cases that most would agree should not result in the defendant taking classes for six months to a year. I represented a woman once who pushed her husband down on a couch. He called the police, and she was cited for DV assault. I have also had many cases where people break their own property and are charged with DV criminal damage.

I have probably had a dozen cases where someone throws his or her own phone and gets charged with criminal damage. Although we do not want people throwing their own phones, do we want people having criminal convictions because of it? I have also handled many cases where other items such as plates get broken, and the person who broke them gets charged.

One other huge issue with DV cases is that many police departments have a policy that if they respond to a DV call, someone has to go to jail. The reasoning is that it is better to arrest someone than not arrest him or her only to have something horrible occur. I have had many cases where the police arrest the wrong person or even just arrest the man in cases where they cannot establish what actually happened.

Even when the police try to do a good job and get to the bottom of the situation, it is hard to figure out what is going on. A lot of the time, both parties are either drunk, on drugs, or so angry that it is hard to figure out what is going on. Sometimes, there will be independent witnesses to help the police sort things out, but this is the exception, not the norm.

Sometimes, it is easy to tell what occurred, and there is a clear guilty party. I have had more than one case where someone was beaten by a rope or extension cord. The pictures of the victims were hard to look because they were bleeding profusely.

As you might expect, many DV cases involve disputes over kids. In a typical case, the couple has split up and is sharing custody of the kid(s), a problem comes up, and the police get involved. I have seen DV cases arise because of the following reasons:

1. "She was supposed to have the kids back to me by 5 p.m., and they didn't get here until 5:30.
2. "He is a terrible dad and doesn't take good care of my kids."
3. "She is mad about the settlement and is using this to get back at me."
4. "He is jealous about my new relationship."

A lot of the time, not only are kids involved but so are other family members. Often, the parents of one of the people in the relationship are somehow involved and only make things worse. There is typically a bad history between the defendant and the family. I had a recent trial that demonstrated this well.

I was representing a young man who had been charged with disorderly conduct. He had gone to his own house after an argument and found his father-in-law at the house. The father-in-law was there fixing a door that the defendant had broken earlier in the day. The father-in-law and my client got into an argument and pleasantries were exchanges. This is the exact conversation that was had:

Defendant: "I know you're scared of me, old man."
Father-in-law: "I ain't scared of you; you're drunk. Leave."
Defendant: "Come at me, you tweaker mother fucker."
Father-in-law: "Nah."

The mother-in-law called the police, and the police responded to where my client was staying. He told them he was upset and tried to fight the police. He told them to pepper spray him and started charging at them. This is a good way to get shot, and he was lucky that he was not. They pepper sprayed him, and he calmed down enough to tell them that he had eight beers.

When I was assigned to the case, my client told me that the father-in-law was making everything up and that he wanted a trial and was innocent. We had a trial, and this was where things got strange. The fact that the judge believed the parents over my guy was not the strange part. The strange part was that my defendant challenged the prosecutor to a drinking contest while he was on the witness stand. The following is the exact conversation between the two:

> Prosecutor: "Sir, you mean to tell me you were sober when you went to your house, but had eight beers by the time the police showed up?"
>
> Defendant: "Yes."
>
> Prosecutor: "You want us to believe you had eight beers in about ten minutes? That seems hard to believe."
>
> Defendant: "You give me some beer right now and I can show you how fast I can drink."
>
> Prosecutor: "That won't be necessary."

At this point, I just put my head down. Things only got worse from there. (I was not sure that was possible.) During sentencing, my client volunteered to the judge that he had cocaine in his system. My client's wife was also on probation for a DV offense, and they were both doing anger management and DV classes for a CPS case in which they were trying to get their child back from the government. All of this demonstrates that there is a tremendous amount of gray areas in the system.

Two felony cases I had several years ago also demonstrate how things are not always as they appear. This is a crucial area of DV cases that new defense lawyers must understand. I represented a young man once who—on paper—had sex with an underage girl by getting her drunk to have sex with her and then hitting her over the head. The reality was very different. The two had met a party, and she lied about her age (not a legal justification, but he had asked). She was not very intoxicated when they met and they were drinking together. She should not have been drinking since she was on several very powerful antipsychotic medications, the labels of which clearly stated they should not be mixed with alcohol.

Later that night, she told him she wanted to have sex with him in the shower. He was drunk too, and it did not seem like a terrible idea to him. As they were having sex in the shower, she fell out of the shower and hit her head on the toilet. She was not badly injured, but there was a lot of blood. My client called the police—who, in turn, arrested him.

At the pretrial, the girl showed up in pigtails, a summer dress, and a big cross around her neck. She was trying to present a very different image than the one he portrayed when she was lying about her age and mixing alcohol and medications.

My point is not that he was right or that she was wrong, but that there was a lot of gray area. I also remember that case because at one of the court hearings, the parents of both kids threatened to burn down each other's trailers.

The second case involved a dragon. My defendant was working as a bouncer in a popular and busy night club. All night he had been flirting with two very attractive women. They came up to him when it was almost closing time and asked him if he wanted to come home with them. His mom did not raise a fool, as he told me, so he said "yes."

As they were leaving the club, the two beautiful women were joined by a third friend. My client was not attracted to the third friend, finding her unattractive. When the women got to their house, they told my client that he had to have sex with the unattractive friend. At this point, my client figured out that this was an elaborate setup to get someone to have sex with the woman he was not attracted to.

My client was confused and told the women he had no interest in having sex with the lady he was not attracted to, and that he needed to go out to his car to get his cigarettes. After returning to the house for a few minutes, the cops showed up. The cops said that the 911 caller had sexually assaulted the three women, and they were scared.

According to the women, they waited for my client to go get his cigarettes to call the police because they were scared for their lives. Even though none of the women had any injuries, the bouncer was still charged—just based on their testimony. My client was facing prison because these women were mad at him. He had never been in trouble and was now facing prison. It took almost six months, but we were eventually able to get the charges dismissed. My defendant learned his lesson.

Assault

As one might guess, there are a huge number of fights in bars and clubs. The more people drink, the worse their decisions become, and things go downhill from there. I have lost track of how many defendants I have represented who were involved in a bar fight. Often, the fights are just with fists, but sometimes someone will really lose his or her senses and pull out a knife or gun.

I represented a defendant once who lost his mind after being kicked out of a strip club. He had gotten drunk inside the strip club and become grabby with one of the dancers. The bouncers kicked him out. He left for a while and then came back and tried fighting the bouncers. The bouncers won the fight, and the defendant said he was going to go to his car, get his gun, and kill everyone. Fortunately for everyone, the police showed up before that, and he was arrested.

Bar fights are a little bit like unsportsmanlike conduct penalties in football. In football, it is not the guy who starts the altercation who gets the penalty, but the guy who retaliates. I have represented many defendants who did not start the fight but they were charged with assault anyway.

Today, many of the clubs and bars have video cameras—which makes it easier to decipher what actually happened. I have defendants who have told me they were just minding their own business when someone hit them. When we the view the video, it was clear that my client was the aggressor. Other times, the bouncers were more of a problem than a solution. I have had several cases where the bouncers escalated the situation and made things worse. If one is a bouncer and one is challenging people to fights, then one is probably not doing one's job right. Sometimes, the bouncers just have a drinking problem.

Last year, I represented a young man who was charged with assault after a street fight. According to my client, he was outside a club where he worked as a bouncer. He saw some guys yelling at a girl. He went over and asked if everything was okay. At that point, one of the guys punched him in the face, so he punched him back. Unfortunately for us, the independent witnesses told a very different story.

According to witnesses, my client came up to a stranger and punched him in the face. He punched the guy so hard that the guy fell to the ground unconscious. We had a trial, and the judge found my defendant guilty. Now, my client has an assault conviction on his record.

Weapons

As you might expect, gun crime is a huge problem in any major city. In Phoenix, Arizona, where everyone is incredibly pro-gun, the problem is even bigger since we have so many residents with guns. We are also blessed with genius legislature that allows people to bring guns into bars. If there is one thing that creates defense work, it is guns and alcohol. In addition, no concealed weapons permit is required to carry a concealed gun in Arizona.

A large part of the problem with guns is that there are some people who have guns and should not. One large group of such people are called prohibited possessors. Different states deal with prohibited possessors in different ways, but virtually every state gives the defined group extra prison time in one way or another.

Prohibited possessors are generally people who have been convicted of a felony and are not allowed to own weapons. Prohibited possessors can receive two years in prison on top of their sentence if they get caught with a gun.

Another common problem defense lawyers see with hand guns are young people using them to either get street cred or just to feel tough. Any defense lawyer who has done a decent amount of felony work has represented at least one young person who was charged with shooting someone at a party. Generally, there is some kind of disagreement and someone will start shooting. Other times, the aggrieved party will leave and come back and do a drive-by shooting at the house. Those types of cases are often a nightmare for prosecutors, as it is very difficult to determine who the shooter was. Imagine a house party with several hundred people, and the shooter is described as a young male in his late teens. Good luck trying to figure out who had the gun and who did the shooting.

Sometimes, the weapons used are not common items. I remember a lawyer telling me that he represented a client who attacked a man with a live snake. The two got into an argument and it turned physical. At one point, one guy took the other guy's snake out of its cage and started using it as a chain to hit the other guy. The snake was about three-feet long, and I am sure it did not enjoy being swung around. I do not remember if the snake was hurt but it did bite the guy who was being hit with it. There should be a rule that you cannot get hit with your own snake.

I have had several clients who have used vibrators and dildos as weapons. I had a case where a woman attacked her boyfriend with a vibrator. The attack was bad enough to leave light bruising and swelling on his body. It had to be difficult to explain to his coworkers how he got attacked with a vibrator.

Scams

In the movie, *The Thomas Crown Affair,* Pierce Brosnan plays a bored billionaire who steals priceless art in amazing and intricate ways only to give the art back later. My defendants are not like that. Most of the scams my clients run are crude and not well thought out and they do not give the objects back later.

One of the most common scams is to use receipts to "return" things you did not buy. The scam has several variations, but they all work in the same general manner. A person goes into a store and picks out an item to take to customer service. The person has an old receipt for the same item. They take the unpaid item and the receipt and try to "return" the item, as if they had already bought it. Most large businesses have caught onto the scam and more and more people are getting caught and prosecuted.

The cousin of the fake return scam is the switching prices scam. A customer will take an expensive price off an item and put a less expensive price sticker on the item. For example, they will take a thirty-dollar piece of clothing and put a ten-dollar tag on it. If they are able to buy the item for ten dollars, they may keep it or they may sell it to someone else for fifteen dollars, making a small profit.

One other common clothing-related scam is walking into a store in one pair of shoes, putting on another pair, and walking out in the new pair without paying for them. A slight variation of the shoe switch is the clothing switch. A person walks into a store in his or her old clothes and takes a bunch of new clothes into the dressing room and tries to leave the store in the new clothes. Sometimes, people will put on the new clothes underneath their old clothes. The problem is that most large stores know who looks suspicious and who to watch on video.

Sometimes, people do not put any thought into stealing clothes. A lawyer peer of mine prosecuted a man who walked into a department store, selected seven leather coats, and ran out of the store. The police got a call that there was a guy running with seven leather coats. It was not hard for the police to find him because he was the only person running with seven leather coats.

The same colleague once prosecuted a guy who tried stealing a refrigerator. The guy walked into the store and used a dolly to wheel the refrigerator out. As he was loading it into the truck, a nice employee offered to help. The fridge was too large for one person to load so the guy stealing it did need help. As they were loading the fridge, the employee just happened to ask for a receipt. It did not take long for the employee to figure out that the fridge was being stolen.

Another equally elaborate scam involves employees stealing from the register. Many of them try to steal small amounts in the hopes that the business does not notice. The money has to be reconciled against receipts at the end of the night, but once in a while the employee who is stealing is able to talk his or her way out of why the receipts and the total of cash do not add up. Other times, he or she winds up as my client.

One of the oldest and most prevalent scams that has been around forever involves people selling their food stamps. The person with the food stamps sells them for cash for some amount less than the face value. The person selling the food stamps gets cash, and the person buying the food stamps can buy food for a lot less than if they were to pay cash. I have seen different exchange rates varying from thirty cents on the dollar to seventy cents on the dollar. In other words, for every food stamp dollar you sell, the person gives you thirty cents in cash. If the people are caught, they are prosecuted for welfare fraud. The people doing the scam not only face the penalty of jail but also lose their ability to get food stamps in the future.

Sometimes, the scams are little more thought out, but the end result is often the same. Many of the half-baked scams involve checks. A young man was enrolled at a major university and his dad was nice enough to pay for his tuition. Every term the dad would give the son a check for tuition, the son would take the check to the school and pay for tuition.

At some point, someone at the school realized there was something fishy about the checks and began an investigation. They figured out the checks were fake and not associated with the account they were supposed to be associated with. When the son went to go pay the next time, he was met by the police who wanted to know why he was committing check fraud. The kid knew nothing about what his dad was doing. The kid was able to avoid criminal charges but did get kicked out of school. What is that old saying about the sins of the father?

One of the funniest check fraud clients I ever had was writing his own U.S. Treasury checks. The fakes were of decent quality with one problem. One time he went to the bank to cash one of his own fake checks when the cashier noticed something on the checks. He had misspelled "United" on the checks. The checks read: "UNTED STATES TREASURY." It did not take Sherlock Holmes to solve this mystery. It is important to remember to run spell-check when committing felony check fraud.

Oftentimes, the people who commit check fraud are so used to writing bad or phony checks that they forget who they are trying to pay. Several years ago, I was representing someone charged with check fraud. He was doing the old scam where he used solvents to take the ink off the check and write different information. He came to my office to pay and wanted to pay me with a personal check.

When I told him that I would not accept a personal check from him, he seemed legitimately confused and even asked me why I would not take the check. I did not want to explain to him that I was pretty sure it was a fake check, so I told him it was my firm's policy not to accept personal checks.

Grand Theft Auto

Car theft is a major issue in any modern urban area. According to a story in the Arizona Republic published several years ago, 13,132 vehicles, or about 308 cars per 100,000 residents, were stolen in the greater Phoenix Area. The numbers were actually an improvement from ten years ago because in 2002, 1,089 cars per 100,000 residents were stolen.

People steal cars for a variety of reasons. One of the most common reasons is money. An experienced car thief knows where to take a stolen car to have it scrapped for parts. As Arizona is close to the Mexican border, some of the cars stolen here will be shipped to Mexico. Getting the cars across the border is not easy, but there are ways. Sometimes, the cars are loaded onto ships or containers. Other times, the cars might be taken apart and reassembled when they reach their destination.

A car will usually be stolen to help with some other crimes. A common example is stealing a car to commit an armed robbery. After the robbery, the car can be abandoned, making it harder for the police to figure out who used the car.

If you steal a car to commit a crime, it is very important to remember to dump the car.

I represented a young man who stole a car to commit some very serious felonies, including armed robbery. Unfortunately for him, he forgot to get rid of the car. When the police found out where he was staying, they also found the stolen car in his garage. Now, on top of all his other charges, he also had a grand theft auto charge.

Sometimes, the car is stolen just so that the person stealing it can go for a joyride and abandon the car in a few hours or a few days. The penalty for stealing a car in Arizona can be years in prison, so there is a high cost to pay for a few hours of joyriding. I have talked to young people (usually men) who stole a car to go joyriding and have been caught. Looking back, they would not have stolen the car—but perhaps they are just saying that because they got caught.

Technology continues to help deter car thefts—while also helping them. As more and more cars are linked to GPS navigation and other tracking technology, it is becoming harder and harder to steal car. Many cars now have computers that can tell when someone is trying to break into the car. Once an intrusion is sensed, the car cannot be started. Many of the cars will also automatically contact the owner to let him or her know there is a possible problem. Other cars have technology so that they can be turned off remotely. For example, your car is stolen, you can call the car company's remote service, and they can turn the car off from thousands of miles away. The days of sticking a screwdriver into the ignition are long gone.

As cars have becoming high tech, so have some car thieves. A smart car thief can start a car with nothing more than a laptop. Today's modern car is basically a giant computer that is connected to the Internet. Anything connected to the Internet can be hacked into wirelessly. A hacker can now unlock and start a car while being miles away from a car.

Bad Driving

I represented a young man who thought it would be a good idea to try to do doughnuts in his sports car around a minivan full of kids. When the prosecutor wanted him to serve a few days in jail to give him time to think about it, he was shocked. His justification was that if the kids had come out of the minivan, he would have slowed down.

Many people are just bad drivers. Some are criminally bad at driving. Some people will sideswipe a parked car or drive off the highway into a ditch. The really strange thing is that these people are often sober. Many of these driving issues involve a distracted driver.

I have had people get cited for reckless or aggressive driving while doing any combination of the following things.

1. Putting on makeup
2. Changing clothes
3. Curling their hair
4. Reading a book
5. Reading a newspaper
6. Eating
7. Yelling at their kids
8. Texting
9. Masturbating (Yes, this is real.)

As you might expect, cell phone use while driving continues to be a major safety concern. Many people talk on their phones, which is dangerous enough, but now many people text while driving, as well? The people texting are easy to spot because their car will usually drift in their own lane and sometimes out of it. I have talked to many officers who thought they were following a drunk driver only to realize that someone was on their phone. More and more states are developing anti-texting laws.

As you can imagine, many bad driving cases involve people racing their cars. Sometimes, the racing is organized. Young men watch *Fast and Furious* one time too many and go drag racing on the streets. Street racing is incredibly dangerous for several reasons. First, they are racing on public streets with everything from pedestrians, to other cars, to objects in the road. Second, most of these drivers do not know how to drive well, and many are young drivers. Third, many times the cars that are being raced are not only unsafe for racing, but unsafe for driving as well.

When you combine all these factors, horrible accidents can happen. I have seen police reports that involved kids who were racing, and the results were everything from severe injuries to death. The second main type of racing is when a race is not planned, but two people just start racing. Often, these types of races are even more dangerous, as there is road rage involved. When you are racing your buddy, you want to win. When you are racing someone you do not know and you have road rage, your judgment is clouded even more. I have represented many people charged with racing, and many of them are fortunate to only lose their cars.

When you are poor, everything is more difficult. Having a working car is just another issue that people with little or no money have to contend with. One issue involving not having a working car comes into play as something as simple as being unable to go to court. Phoenix Metro is a huge area, and many of my defendants have to travel a long way to make it to court. It is not unusual for one of my clients to have to travel thirty to fifty miles one way to get to court.

I estimate that I have at least one defendant a week who misses court because of car issues. Sometimes, their own car does not work. Other times, they are supposed to get a ride from someone and that person has car trouble. Not having a car that works is a part of the vicious cycle that many defendants get themselves into due to their financial situation.

When a client is not able to make it to court, a warrant is put on him or her. Now, they not only have the original charge but, on top of that, a warrant also. Sometimes, the person will get arrested on the warrant and put in jail. If he or she has money for bail, he or she is out of even more money as a result of the bail. If a person does not have money for bail, he or she sits in jail and risk losing his or her jobs. Most of us take our cars for granted, but for many of my defendants, a lack of a working car is a constant issue.

Not having a properly working car can also result in criminal charges. Oftentimes, my defendants are pulled over for not having a properly working car. The infraction can range from a broken windshield, to a nonworking turn signal, to no license plate light.

The police will usually use these minor infractions as an excuse to pull someone over. Once someone is pulled over, the police can look for other crimes to charge the driver or occupants with. A typical case might involve someone who is pulled over for having a burnt out brake light bulb, and then the officer finds drugs in the car. I have even had people get pulled over on bicycles for not having proper lighting.

Chapter Five

Defense Lawyers

Defense lawyers are an interesting group of people. Just like judges and prosecutors and police, no two are the same, and they have their individual quirks. There are some similarities that most defense lawyers do have in common. Most share a belief that people's basic constitutional rights have to be protected.

A common saying among defense lawyers is that we defend not only the individual, but the entire system of the Constitution and checks and balances. One of the most common questions I hear from my nondefense lawyer friends is, what does your job entail and what do you do all day?

A Day in the Life

The good and bad part of being a defense lawyer is that you are not stuck behind a desk all day. Defense lawyers spend a lot of time in the courtroom or driving back and forth between the courts. Last year, I drove twenty thousand miles. I have defense lawyer friends who will drive anywhere from thirty thousand miles to fifty thousand miles in one year. The reason the mileage adds up so quickly is that many of the courts are far from each other and many judges want the lawyer to be present—even for matters that can easily be done over the phone, or via fax or e-mail. I take cases in one court that is one hundred seventy miles outside of Phoenix. I have made the drive for a five-minute continuance because the judge insisted I be present: one hundred seventy miles to get there, a five-minute hearing, and one hundred seventy miles back.

Even within town, many of the courts are far apart. I have had days when I drove over two hundred miles within one town, just driving from court to court. Sometimes, I will start the morning in one court and have to drive forty miles across town to another court, just to come back to the same court I started at. Some lawyers also have to drive to some of the Arizona Department of Corrections prisons that are spread all over the place.

When a defense lawyer is not driving, he or she is often sitting. Sitting and waiting is a big part of the job. We are usually waiting for court to start. If a judge is running late, you cannot call the judge and tell him or her to hurry up. You have to sit there and wait. I can generally tell when someone is an experienced lawyer because he or she will have a book or newspaper with him or her. If we are not waiting for a judge, we may be waiting for an in-custody defendant to be brought over. I have spent time waiting for my defendant to be transported to my courtroom, so his or her case could be dismissed. A two-minute dismissal has ended up taking well over an hour.

Get Used to Waiting

Another place where a lot of waiting takes place is in the jails and prisons. First, you wait to be let in, then you wait to see your defendant, and then you wait to be let out. There is a lot of waiting when things are going well. You can probably imagine how long of a wait there is when things are not going well. I have been in jails when there was an "incident" and the entire facility was locked down. This was not fun for me, as I was inside the jail and could not get out for several hours.

Another time, I was in the jail and the correctional officers forgot about me. There is a button to push to call someone, but if no one is on the other end, you are stuck. Cell phones are not allowed in the jails (for obvious reasons), so there is no way to call for help. Once I drove several hours to a prison to see an inmate just to have the prison staff tell me it would be a couple of hours before they could let me in. I had a defense lawyer friend who was visiting a client and while inside the jail there was a security lockdown and no one was allowed to enter or leave the building. My friend had to sit in the hallway for over five hours until the all clear signal was given.

Getting locked in the jail is always a potential perk of the job. Sometimes, it is more fun than others. I was representing a young man who had committed a number of violent felonies and I had visited him at the jail and played some video clips for him. The facility where he was being held was a maximum security facility, reserved for the worst of the worst criminal offenders. Normally at this facility, you meet your clients in a little room with acrylic glass dividing you from your client.

On this occasion, I had to have my laptop with me to play the video for him, so they let me into a special room. The room was inside the jail and could only be opened with a key. This meant that I was locked inside the room with my client. After I was locked in the room, the correctional officers left and told me to let them know when I was done. Being in a locked room with a violent client with no guards around is a challenge to one's nerves. I remember wondering how many minutes it would take the guards to get there if something happened, and wondering how many times I could be stabbed with a pen during those minutes. Of course, nothing happened, but I was nervous nonetheless.

Interpersonal Skills

Driving and waiting are large parts of the job, but the biggest aspect involves talking to people. All day, I am either talking to my defendants, to prosecutors, or to judges.

If you do not like to talk, it will be hard if not impossible to be a successful defense lawyer.

Some lawyers have offices in which they meet clients, whereas others just meet their clients in courthouses and coffee shops. I like meeting my clients outside the office simply for scheduling purposes. If I set a meeting with a client or potential client at my office and he or she does not show up (which happens incredibly often), I have wasted my own time. If I have to be in court at 8:30 a.m. and I schedule a meeting with a client at 8:00 a.m. outside that courthouse and he or she does not show up, I get to enjoy a quiet cup of coffee while meeting my next obligation.

I cannot stress enough the importance of strong interpersonal skills. Regardless of if you work for a government agency or are in private practice, the importance of developing strong communication skills will have a direct effect on your career. A large part of what defense lawyers do is talk to people. We talk to bailiffs, clerks, prosecutors, judges, other defense lawyers, clients, witnesses, investigators, and anyone else that may be involved with a case. If you cannot communicate well with all these people, you will be ill equipped to be a defense lawyer.

Although some people are fortunate to have naturally strong interpersonal skills, most people have to work on them and practice. I believe that interpersonal skills should constantly be worked on. Think of them as you would with any other skills. If you want to get good at playing the piano, you have to practice for hours with that piano. If you want to develop strong interpersonal skills, you need to work on them in a similar time fashion. Having strong interpersonal skills will help you in your ability to communicate, but they will also make you more money by bringing you more clients and better results for your clients. Sometimes, the person who decides to hire me will ask for my services right after we have had a good conversation. Sometimes, referrals come from the clerk at the court who assigns me extra cases because I am friendly, respectful, and always talk to her and listen to her. If you are a defense lawyer and are shy, introverted, and hate talking to people, this will also have an effect on your potential income.

The Ability to Manage Time, Schedules, and Judges

One other major aspect of being a defense lawyer is having to be in several places at the same time. I once had four trials going on at the same time. I would not recommend this to new defense lawyers. An organized schedule can help reduce the amount of times you have to be in two or three places at the same time, but it does not solve the problem completely. I have been in front of judges who do not care that I have a scheduling conflict.

Some judges will tell defense lawyers that their schedule is their problem and that they need to figure it out. Sometimes, courts are more flexible, but problems still come up. Court dates get mixed up, or things get set on the wrong days. I have experienced several occasions when the court set something on the wrong day and then called me asking me why I am not at the court. To be fair, I have also made calendar errors and shown up on the wrong date. I remember that I once showed up to court a week early. Better early than late.

Buddy System Beware

Defense lawyers will often ask their friends to stand in for them when they cannot be somewhere. I will call my defense lawyer friends, ask them to stand in, and hope that I am not throwing them on a landmine. Sometimes, you think the court date will be smooth and simple so you send someone in your place, but when that person shows up, all hell breaks loose.

Sometimes, a lawyer knows he or she is throwing a fellow lawyer on a landmine but does not say anything. I was an inexperienced lawyer and did not know up from down. A defense lawyer friend asked me to cover a sentencing for her. She told me it was a stipulated plea and all I had to do was show up. In reality, the plea was not stipulated and there was a ten-year range. The defendant could get anywhere from ten to twenty years in prison.

When I showed up, there was a full courtroom, and everyone was crying. The defendant was naturally freaked out as he was expecting his regular lawyer there. Instead, he saw a young man who was clearly fresh out of law school.

Everything turned out fine and the defendant got the minimum ten years, but it was still a scary experience for me and the defendant.

Advertising, Fees and Getting Paid

The traditional business model for defense lawyers in private practice had always been simple. Open an office, get clients, and have clients pay for your services. Not that long ago, many lawyers did not advertise and not that long before that, most state bar organizations did not allow lawyers to advertise because it was seen as demeaning to a lawyer to advertise.

Over time, it became harder for defense lawyers to obtain private clients. The reason for the change is twofold. First, there are many more lawyers than there used to be. At some point, for a variety of reasons, lots of people decided to go to law school, though the decline in law school enrollments over the past decade has reduced the total number of lawyers. However, with lawyer work scares, as more people graduated from law school, they started their own practice and began competing with other lawyers for clients. The pie did not become bigger, but the slices got smaller.

Second, more and more clients convinced themselves they could take care of their own legal matters on their own either through online research or document provider companies. If a document prep company tells you that it can give you all the forms you need for two hundred dollars and a lawyer says his or her fee is two thousand dollars, it is easy to see how someone might be tempted do go with the document prep company. In the long run, people get themselves into more trouble with the forms, but that is a different discussion for a different time.

All of that being said, the market for lawyers is not as bad as it was when I started my practice in 2009. Although I still believe that it is hard to succeed today as a lawyer, it is not as bad as it was. Some lawyers think there is a ray of hope as many baby boomer lawyers approach retirement. The hope is that once the baby boomer lawyers retire, there will be more positions opening up for new lawyers. The problem with this assumption is that many baby boomer lawyers cannot afford to retire and will have to keep working. Only time will tell how many baby boomer lawyers actually retire in the next several years.

As getting clients became harder and harder, lawyers began to advertise more and more. The original ads were in phone books, on the radio, or on church bulletins. With the growth of the Internet, the ads moved to websites and online marketing. Today, I know lawyers spending tens of thousands of dollars a month just on advertising.

A lawyer must have a website nowadays. Not that long ago, a defense lawyer could get away with not having a website, but those days are gone. Today, when I have referral clients, they are still going to my website to check me out.

Rates and Fees

The rates that criminal defense lawyers charge vary widely from lawyer to lawyer. A good example is among the DUI lawyers in Phoenix. I know lawyers who will take a first offense DUI cases for less than one thousand dollars, whereas others will charge ten thousand dollars for the exact same case. The rules that govern lawyer conduct say that a fee has to be "reasonable," but "reasonable" is a subjective term.

I have a very good friend who charges ten thousand dollars for a DUI case for the simple reason that he can. He is one of the best DUI lawyers in Arizona, and when a person with money gets a DUI, he or she calls him. An interesting trend among clients that I have noticed is that they equate the quality of their lawyer with how much they paid. A client who pays a lawyer five thousand dollars thinks that his or her lawyer is better than a lawyer who charges three thousand dollars. This is sometimes true—but not always. I have even heard clients argue about whose lawyer was better based on how much each person paid their lawyer.

Getting a client to agree to pay for my services and actually getting him or her to pay are two very different things. This is the reason that one of the golden rules of criminal defense work is to get the money up front.

First, a client will usually not want to pay once the case is over. It does not matter if we have a signed fee agreement (which we always do) or how good of a job I did for him or her. No one ever wants to pay once the case is over. I have had clients try to explain to me that they do not need to pay since the case is over and I am no longer working on their case. I always appreciated that logic and it reinforced my "money up front" requirement.

Second, some clients who have experience in the system know that once their lawyer files a notice of appearance, a judge may not let them off the case. Some clients will actually have a strategy where they will do anything to get the lawyer to file a notice of appearance, knowing that the lawyer may be stuck with their case once the paperwork is filed. Once a notice of appearance is filed, a judge has to agree to let the lawyer off the case. If the judge does not let the lawyer off the case, the lawyer is stuck. Sometimes, the lawyer is stuck doing the case for free.

I had a potential client call me once and say he wanted to hire me. I could tell the client was fishy because I usually have good instinct about this. He told me that he had hired a different lawyer but did not like that lawyer and wanted to hire me instead. I knew the other lawyer and knew he was not the greatest at his job, and it was possible that this defendant actually did need new counsel. I told the potential client that—once I got paid—I would file a substitution of counsel, making me the lawyer of record and excusing the prior lawyer.

As a courtesy, I called the lawyer who was already on the case. He told me that he had not yet been paid but had already filed a notice of appearance. The other lawyer had made a huge mistake and had fallen into the trap set by the client. The lawyer was now stuck with the client, and I suspect the lawyer will never get paid.

Once I receive some money up front, I will do payment plans, but I have to know that the money I get up front may be the only money I ever see. For example, if I tell a client that a DUI case will be four thousand dollars, and he or she gives me one thousand five hundred dollars up front, I have to be fine with doing the case for one thousand five hundred dollars as a risk of the business. Sometimes, my clients do not want to pay me, and other times they are simply not able to.

Some lawyers will sue their clients for any money owed. I never liked the idea of suing my own clients because it is generally more trouble than it is worth. Not only is it not worth my time, but agitating a client tends to have negative consequences. One consequence that has developed is the influence of the Internet as a vehicle for unhappy clients to leave negative reviews on websites. One bad review can have a direct impact on a lawyer's income.

Is the couple of hundred or even couple of thousand dollars you may eventually win worth getting smeared over the Internet? I also consider not getting paid my own fault. If I do work without getting paid for it, that is on me. If I let a client take advantage of a payment plan and do not do anything about it before it is too late, that is on me.

Having private clients is a core component of a defense attorney's case file. The problem with relying on private clients alone is twofold. First, there is an insane amount of competition among defense lawyers for clients. I focus much of my private work on DUI cases. I know that there are probably close to three hundred other defense lawyers in the greater Phoenix area competing for the same clients. That means that every time someone hires me, I have to beat out three hundred other lawyers.

Competing for Clients, Advertising

Entire books have been written on the subject of lawyer advertising. The goal of this section is not a thorough analysis of every issue relating to lawyer advertising but to point out several main ideas. Today, when I get a call from a potential client, it is not unusual for him or her to have spoken to three or five other lawyers. I know this because he or she tells me. Oftentimes, the client asks me if I can beat some other lawyer's price. Oftentimes, I know the lawyer with the enticing low ball quote and I know that he or she cannot lawyer his way out of a paper bag. For obvious reasons, I cannot tell the potential client that the other lawyer he or she spoke to is not a very good lawyer. I have to try to convince potential clients to hire me without bad-mouthing other lawyers. Never bad-mouth other lawyers to potential clients. You will be amazed at how quickly your remarks will get back to the lawyer in question. This has happened several times to lawyers I know and it is always a huge mess.

There is not only huge competition between lawyers for clients, but there is also great competition among advertisers for lawyer advertising dollars. There are no less than ten advertising companies that call me all the time, trying to get me to advertise with them. Some of the companies flat-out lie about what they can do. I know the companies are lying because I have had friends advertise with those companies and lots of promises were made, but no results were delivered.

If a lawyer does not know a lot about advertising, it is easy for the advertiser to make insane promises to get the lawyer excited. When deciding where to advertise, the best idea is always to talk to other lawyers who have tried the spot that you are thinking about. It is better to learn from someone else's mistakes than your own. Also, remember that what works for one lawyer may not necessarily work for a different lawyer. For example, some defense lawyers have told me they still get clients from phone book ads, whereas others tell me it is a total waste of money.

The second problem with relying solely on private clients is that there will always be upward and downward swings in the number of clients you get. I have had weeks during which I get three new private clients, and I have had months where I had no new private clients. Any experienced criminal lawyer will tell you that the flow of clients is rarely steady. There are some incredibly well-established lawyers who have a fairly steady flow of lawyers, but even they will tell you that some months are better than others.

Different Types of Defense Lawyers

Just like with prosecutors, there are certain personality types that are visible among defense lawyers. As noted earlier in Chapter One, the trait that all defense lawyers share is a belief that everyone's rights have to be protected. I have never met a defense lawyer who did not agree with this principle. All defense lawyers stand up for people who have no one else on their side. Although all defense lawyers protect the individual rights of their clients as guaranteed by the Constitution, this next group of lawyers can border on fanatical.

True Believers

The first type of defense lawyer is the true believer. Just as the true believer prosecutor believes that everyone is guilty, the true believer defense lawyer believes that everyone is innocent. Many true believer defense lawyers will also believe that all police are corrupt and all prosecutors cannot tell right from wrong. Just as with prosecutors, this is a small but vocal minority.

I think that although defense lawyers should believe in protecting their clients, they must also pick and choose their battles. Not every prosecutor is out to deprive your client of their rights. Not every client was wronged by the police. You can fight for your client and still realize this.

True believer defense lawyers are incredibly passionate, which is good. They are also often unreasonable, which is bad. I have heard these lawyers talk to prosecutors, and it often goes something like this:

> True believer defense lawyer: "Why are you trying to screw my client and deprive her of her Constitutional rights?"
>
> Prosecutor: "I don't think that's what I am doing. Your client has thirteen prior convictions for shoplifting, and I am asking for ten days jail. Technically, I could dismiss this misdemeanor charge and file it as a felony, but I don't think that is appropriate. Your client can't just keep stealing stuff."
>
> True believer defense lawyer: "That's what a Nazi prosecutor would say!"
>
> Prosecutor: "Huh? What?"

Both prosecutors and defense lawyers do not like working with counterparts that are true believers. They want to fight issues that are not actually issues, and often make things a lot more personal than they need to be. I remember one altercation between a prosecutor and a true believer defense lawyer that clearly illustrated this.

I was working in jail court and the assigned prosecutor was one of the most honest, reasonable, and compassionate people I have ever worked with. The other defense lawyer was a true believer. The prosecutor was asking for a bond for a defendant who had failed to appear in court on many occasions. The defense lawyer was angry that the prosecutor would seek a bond—even though it was totally reasonable.

The defense lawyer began to personally attack the prosecutor because of this and was acting very irrational.

This lawyer was also famous for believing her clients when it was obvious to everyone, except her, that they were lying. A good defense lawyer should have a well-honed ability to see through bullshit. A true believer defense lawyer will often believe the client at any cost. For true believer defense lawyers, a scorched earth approach is the only way. In the end, the clients represented by such a true believer find themselves under worse terms of incarceration than a defense attorney with respect for the prosecutor and self-awareness about their own case.

I have a true believer defense lawyer friend who got mad at me when I told her I had lunch with a prosecutor. I was friends with the prosecutor and always thought he did a great job professionally. The lawyer told me that I was having lunch with the enemy and that it was a bad idea. She went on to say that defense lawyers should not be friends with prosecutors, as they are evil and defense lawyers are good. Imagine having that kind of outlook on life.

Lazy or Lost Lawyers

There are also lazy lawyers. When I say lazy, I mean it in two very different ways. The first is that some are lazy about the practice of law. What I mean is that they do not want to work very hard for their clients. These lawyers do the minimum, or sometimes even less, and nothing more. They do this for different reasons, but they do exist. The second type of laziness I see is lawyers who are lazy about the *business* of being lawyers.

There is a group of lawyers who are not happy about how their practice or career is going but refuse to do anything about it. When I talk to these lawyers, they tell me how "lucky" I am to have a successful career. Some of the lawyers in this group refuse to take the steps needed to cultivate their businesses.

Some of these lawyers are new and have never had successful practices. Some are lawyers who have been practicing for a while and used to have successful practices but something changed and now they cannot figure out why the money is no longer coming in.

There is still plenty of opportunity for lawyers to be successful, but the work has to be put in. I have talked to lawyers who are running their practices the same way they were twenty or thirty years ago. The problem is that the legal market and legal marketing have changed drastically in that time.

There are lawyers who refuse to learn new technology and new marketing techniques. The Internet has drastically changed how lawyers market their services and how clients seek legal services. If you are lawyer and your mindset is that you do not need to learn new marketing techniques, you will be in trouble and the practice of law will pass you by. The rate of change is amazing, and lawyers have to keep up to stay relevant and competitive. The old adage about having to evolve or face extinction is very true.

There are also lawyers who are unhappy with where they work but refuse to leave. Many of these lawyers have cushy jobs where the expectations are low, but so is the pay. I have spoken with many of these lawyers who are working for governments or firms, and all of them complain about their pay. I tell them that they can make more in private practice, but there is a lot of more work and a lot more challenges. Many tell me they do not want extra work. As we know, you get out what you put in. There are no miracles.

Another group of defense lawyers is the group that is burned out. They are usually burned out from one of two main reasons—and sometimes a combination of the two. Some are burned out from the work. This makes sense as many defense lawyers take on huge emotional burdens. Imagine spending thirty years defending people who commit unimaginable sex crimes against children. Some defense lawyers are able to cope with the emotional toll of their work better than others, but there is a toll for everyone.

Many defense lawyers who start out doing only felony work eventually transition to more misdemeanor work because as the emotional toll is often less. With a misdemeanor case, if you lose, your client might get a fine or a few days in jail. If you lose a felony case, your client is likely going to prison and sometimes facing the death penalty.

From my own years of practice, I know there is more of an emotional toll with felony work than with misdemeanor work. There is still an emotional toll stemming from misdemeanor work, but it is considerably less so than with felony work. The second main reason lawyers get burned out is an economic reason.

If a lawyer has worked his or her whole career and does not have very much money at the end of the career, this may cause the lawyer to burn out on the practice of law. Many of the reasons people have financial trouble are self-induced. I have spoken to many defense lawyers who look back on their careers and regret the huge amounts of money they wasted on things they did not need.

I spoke to one female lawyer who is in her sixties now and close to broke. She told me that a while ago, when her practice was going well, she spent over ten thousand dollars one year on electronics. It was clear to see that she could really use that money today.

Part of the blame lies with the individual lawyers, but part of the blame also belongs to law schools. Traditionally, law schools have been terrible when it comes to teaching lawyers about money and managing their finances. When lawyers graduate law school, they know the law, but they do not know basic things like how to manage their practice overhead or how to deal with their loans. Law schools are starting to get better by offering classes that teach law students how to manage their practices, but for many lawyers, it is way too late. Law schools need to not only teach the business side of practicing law, but also humility.

Arrogant, Self-Absorbed Defense Lawyers

The next group of lawyers are the arrogant ones. These lawyers are in love with themselves and often have insanely large egos. Unfortunately, there are many of these lawyers. Although every defense lawyer must have some ego and take pride in his or her work, some defense lawyers take it too far. They begin to fall in love with themselves and do not have people in their lives to rein them in.

Some lawyers think that arrogance is good for their career. It is true that some clients like arrogant lawyers because the clients confuse competence with arrogance. A client might wrongly think that if a lawyer is arrogant in court, that lawyer must be really good. Although some of the arrogant lawyers I know are very good lawyers, others are just terrible. In reality, arrogance hurts a lawyer's career a lot more than it helps.

When a lawyer is arrogant, everyone knows. Everyone—including the court staff, the prosecutor, and other defense lawyers—knows it. If a defense lawyer is arrogant with a prosecutor, do you think that prosecutor is going to make a better plea offer or a worse one? This is one of the ways arrogant lawyers hurt their clients. If an arrogant lawyer goes to a prosecutor and tells the prosecutor how awesome he or she is, and how stupid the prosecutor is, this will not help the client. If a lawyer goes in and is humble, polite, and respectful to the prosecutor, the prosecutor is more likely to make a better offer to my client. When you realize this, which type of lawyer would you rather have?

A subset of the arrogant lawyer is the arrogant new lawyer. I see these new lawyers in court all the time. They have no idea what they are doing and are strangely arrogant, despite not knowing what they are doing. I have seen them talk down to people in court. This type of behavior will harm their clients, and their own standing in the legal community both in the short and long term. Many of these fledgling lawyers ruin their own careers before they ever get started.

A defense lawyer who I know started out in the county prosecutor's office and pretty much killed his career there, too. While he was there, he was arrogant and unpleasant and his behavior poisoned the well, so to speak. He left the prosecutor's office and became a defense lawyer, but everyone remembered the things he did as a prosecutor and it hurt his network and his ability to work professionally with prosecutors.

New lawyers are extended a certain amount of slack among prosecutors, judges, and fellow defense attorneys because they are just starting out and people understand that learning takes time. When I was a fledgling lawyer, I would come up to court staff and say, "I am new; I don't know anything. Please, please help me." And guess what? They did help because I did not come to them with arrogance. I see new lawyers who not only have no clue what they are doing but are too arrogant to ask for help. Some of them are actively hurting their clients with their arrogance. Sometimes, the law students do not even wait to get their law licenses to be arrogant.

One of the courts I work in has an intern program that I normally participate in. Every term, a law student is matched up with a defense lawyer so that he or she can shadow that lawyer and learn from him or her. I was sitting around with a defense lawyer friend and we were talking about our respective interns. I was saying how mine was great, worked hard, had a humble attitude, and always did what I asked him to.

My friend told me he was having a different experience with his intern. First, the intern came to court smelling like marijuana. That is strike one, and two. Strike three came when my friend asked the intern to research some legal issue. The intern went to Google and punched in the phrase and printed out the result. You do not have to graduate law school to know that this is not how you do legal research for your supervising lawyer.

I always tell my students that I can forgive honest mistakes. If you make a wrong objection in a trial, that is fine because that is a part of learning. What I cannot forgive with my interns and law students is arrogance and not caring. When you come to court smelling like marijuana and blatantly do not care about a research project that your boss gives you—that is inexcusable. You can see how some new lawyers manage to end their careers before they ever get started.

Lawyers with Substance Abuse Issues

As you must expect, there are also quite a few lawyers with substance abuse issues. I think part of the reason for this is that many lawyers are under tremendous stress, and not very good at dealing with it in healthy ways. Instead of going for a run or doing a yoga class, some lawyers will take pills or drink alcohol.

For many lawyers, the substance issue begins in law school, and things only get worse from there. If you are in law school and you drink too much, you will only increase how much you drink because the amount of stress goes up. I knew people in law school who had drinking problems, and their drinking problems only got worse. As we now know, substance abuse issues rarely go away on their own.

When I teach Professional Responsibility, I make my students write a report on a lawyer who got in trouble with the state bar. The goal of the assignment is for students to see some of the reasons lawyers get themselves in trouble. The students are always surprised how many of the problems lead back to substance abuse. Even when the problem on the surface is not substance related, it often is the problem when you look deeper.

A common reason that lawyers get into trouble is because they mishandled clients' money. Although some lawyers steal from their clients and do not have a substance abuse problem, it seems to be the exception. It seems like every year, there are cases of an Arizona lawyer having a problem with alcohol or drugs. Just last year, a defense lawyer was disbarred after admitting he had a cocaine problem. The lawyer admitted that he would often come to court high. Imagine being a client who is facing prison and your lawyer is high.

There are also cases almost every year involving defense lawyers who are charged with DUIs. Sometimes, the lawyer who is charged focuses his entire practice on DUI defense, so you would think the lawyer would know better. There are also cases of lawyers who have had more than one DUI. Although anyone can have one DUI, once there is a second and third, there is likely a substance abuse issue.

I have seen lawyers' families and practices fall apart because of substance abuse. Sometimes, the problem starts out small and spirals out of control. Sometimes, a person is a heavy drinker and then his or her health goes downhill. A combination of a high-stress career and neglecting one's health by abusing alcohol or drugs is a recipe for disaster.

State bars have gotten better over the years at having programs for lawyers struggling with substance issues. The problem is that many lawyers struggling with these issues are afraid to come forward for fear of losing their law license. If you are a lawyer and lose your law license, that is the end of the road. As a lawyer, your livelihood depends on having a law license.

Dishonest Defense Lawyers

The last type of lawyer that I see, and arguably the worst kind, is the con artist and the liar. These lawyers will do anything and say anything to potential clients to get the individuals to hire them. These lawyers give all lawyers a bad name.

Since the market for defense lawyers is incredibly competitive, some lawyers have figured out an effective method for getting clients. These lawyers guarantee results to potential clients. When a potential client comes in who is charged with a DUI, the lawyer says, "If you hire me, I guarantee a dismissal." When the same client with the same DUI comes to me, I say, "I will do everything I can but can't make any guarantees." Which lawyer do you think the client will go with?

One client told me that he went to the firm to hire a defense lawyer for a friend. The guy meeting with the lawyer told him his relative had a stipulated plea for five years in prison and asked if the lawyer could get him a better deal. The correct answer would be "no." A stipulated plea is exactly what it sounds like. It means the defendant knows his or her sentence. The amount of prison time is stipulated to, and the judge has no discretion to give less or more time with a stipulated plea. What the lawyer actually said was "yes."

The man paid the lawyer five thousand dollars, and the lawyer said he would show up to the sentencing to get a better plea for the relative. On the day of sentencing, a different lawyer from the firm showed up. The different lawyer looked at the plea and told everyone it was a stipulated plea and that nothing could be done. The lawyer then walked out of court and never refunded any of the five thousand dollars.

Unethical firms will use many of the same tactics used by time share sellers. The firm has professional sales people who meet with potential clients. The sales people are paid a percentage of the legal fee, so they will say anything to get the potential clients to sign up. I have talked to clients who meet with these sales people, and many of the promises that were made were nothing short of irresponsible.

One of the grossest tactics these firms used was not letting people leave until they signed up. When a person came in for a consultation, the intake personnel would ask to see the person's driver's license to make a copy for the file. The intake personnel would not give the license back until that person signed up. When the person would ask for his or her license back, he or she was given excuse after excuse until he or she signed up. It was not unusual to keep people in the office for hours.

Putting clients on payment plans that they know the client cannot honor is another terrible practice employed by some defense lawyers. There is always a down payment, and then a payment plan for the remainder amount. Once the client falls behind on the payment plan, as the lawyer is hoping he or she will do, the lawyer goes to the judge and asks to be let off the case. The client loses the down payment, and the lawyer gets paid for doing nothing. Some firms are so bad that I have seen judges catch on and not let a firm off a case. I love it when judges stand up to lawyers who are cheating clients.

Another example of unethical behavior among lawyers is telling clients they have a good case for trial while knowing that this is simply not true. Unethical lawyers do this because they have a trial fee in their agreements with the clients. There is nothing wrong with a separate trial fee, and I charge one myself. The unethical part involves getting your clients' hopes up when you know there is no issue or chance, but tell them there is one.

If the lawyer can convince a client that there is a good issue worth fighting, the client is more likely to pay the trial fee. The setup is a win-win for the lawyer. If the client does pay the trial fee, the lawyer gets paid an additional amount. If the client cannot pay the trial fee but wants to proceed to trial because the lawyer got the client's hopes up, the lawyer withdraws from the case.

I had a client assigned to me on a contract case. He had been represented by one of these lawyers. The client had paid the firm a large amount of money, and when they wanted even more for a trial fee, he could not afford it, so they withdrew from the case. They told him he had a great issue, and he did not. The lawyer who told him he had a great issue was either incompetent or lying.

The issue was whether or not the arresting officer has to explain how a defendant can get a restricted license after their initial license suspension is up as a result of a DUI stop. The obvious answer is that the officer does not. If the officer had to explain every possible eventual license implication to every defendant, a DUI stop could take ten hours. The lawyer had convinced the client that the arresting officer did not go over possible restricted license options, so it was a bad stop and the case should be thrown out.

Now, this client thinks he has a good issue for trial. When I tell him it was not a good issue, he tells me that his last lawyer told him that I would say that since public defenders do not work hard for their clients. So now the old lawyer is not only giving terrible legal advice for monetary gain, but putting down public defenders. Committing two cardinal sins of criminal defense with one client is not easy to do.

Hateful Defense Lawyers

"People who hate you because of a mere jealousy over your success hurt themselves in disguise. This is because you carry an image of who they wish they had become. Don't hate them back because they may also become like you one day and it will mean hurting that image you carry!"

—*Israelmore Ayivor*

Defense lawyers are, in general, a competitive group. All defense lawyers have some ego, and every defense lawyer wants to be successful. For some, success is defined by money. For some, it is defined by reputation or case results. Although most defense lawyers want to see other defense lawyers succeed, some only want to bring other defense lawyers down. It is too often that I see lawyers not doing well themselves, so they seek company in their misery.

As already discussed, there are many unhappy defense lawyers. Some are unhappy because their careers did not work out the way they thought they should. Some are unhappy because they did not make the kind of money they deserved. Yet others are unhappy because someone else is doing well. These lawyers are the haters.

I first realized this phenomenon when I was a newly minted lawyer. I had only been in practice about a year and my practice was not making a lot of money, but I was starting to build my reputation and cultivating my practice. One of my jobs was to cover for lawyers at a glorified help desk. There was a desk in a court and a defense lawyer was paid to sit there and answer questions. The lawyer was not there to fish for private clients but to answer legal questions and point people in the right direction. I worked at that desk a lot and never got a private client out of it. I had never gotten a private client out of it because I had never tried.

One day, a friend of mine told me she heard an older lawyer hating on me. My friend heard the older lawyer gossiping about me to other lawyers and falsely saying I was getting a ton of clients from my work at the help desk. I thought this was strange since, as mentioned, I had never gotten one client from the help desk. As I got to know the older lawyer who was bad-mouthing me, I began to understand why she would do that.

She was not a happy person, and her career had not gone like she thought it should have. She was putting down a fledgling lawyer like me because I was starting to build my practice. The longer I am in practice, the more I see lawyers bad-mouthing other lawyers who are doing well. I had a wonderful friend who was the single hardest working defense lawyer I had ever known. Through incredible hard work, he became very successful and made a lot of money. The more money he made, the more other lawyers tried to drag him down and bad-mouth him behind his back.

I would hear people complain how he had too many cases and ran around too much. They were jealous of his success but not willing to put in the amount of work he had. Defense lawyers never have and never will become successful through luck. Since I was a fledgling lawyer and my friend had been around longer than I had been, I often asked him if it bothered him that people talked so much about him behind his back. He told me that it did not and that he was aware that the more success he had, the more people would hate on him. He believed that trying to change those people was a pointless endeavor.

Now that I have been practicing for a while, I hear of more and more defense lawyers talking about me behind my back. They say the same things they said about my friend. He has too many cases, and he has too many jobs.

My favorite comment I heard someone say about me is, why does he need to try to make so much money?

Some lawyers take their hatred to the next level. One defense lawyer recently filed a bar complaint against a fellow defense lawyer. I cannot get into the specifics of the matter, but the issue was incredibly petty and filing a bar complaint over the issue should be given a gold medal in pedantry. The real reason the lawyer filed the bar complaint is because the lawyer was jealous over the success of the other lawyer. Instead of trying to build up the lawyer's practice, the lawyer was trying to tear other lawyers down.

Frustrating Days

As a defense lawyer, there are many frustrating days, and they are frustrating for different reasons. As you can guess, the clients themselves are causes of much of the frustration. As a defense lawyer, you represent many people who keep making the same mistakes over and over.

I cannot tell you how often I have had clients swear to everyone in the courtroom that they will never get in trouble again—only to be arrested for the same crime several weeks or several months later. It is not unusual for me to represent the same individual for a second and sometimes a third time.

Every defense lawyer has had cases during which they put everything they have into a case and get a great outcome for a client. The client is thrilled and says he or she learned from the experience and will change his or her life. You can guess what happens next. The client gets in trouble for the same thing and all the lawyer's hard work goes to waste.

Oftentimes, the cause of the frustration is clients not appreciating your work. Although no defense lawyer expects a hug and a fruit basket, a thank you often goes a long way. Not only do we not usually get a thank you, but also the clients usually question our work.

I represented a defendant several years ago who committed a hate crime and was clearly guilty. He was a white man who had pointed a loaded rifle at a little African American girl. He admitted to the police that the only reason he did it was because she was black. He did not want to plead guilty, and we had a trial. At the trial, not only did the little girl testify that the rifle was pointed at her but so did some of the neighbors. To the surprise of no one, my client was convicted. After the trial, he told me that if I had done a better job, he could have won the trial.

For defense lawyers, a client's lack of self-reflection is often frustrating. Although some clients take responsibility for their actions, many do not. If someone gets a DUI, it is the fault of everyone except the person charged. It is the fault of the cop for pulling him or her over and the fault of the prosecutor for prosecuting him or her. I am often taken aback when I do have a client who says, "I was wrong; I take full responsibility for my actions."

I have lost track of cases during which people attack their spouses and—when they get arrested—they blame the spouse. If the spouse had not called the police, the attacker would not have gotten in trouble. Many clients fail to see the causal link between their actions and the consequences.

Seeing how much of the system comes down on poor people so hard is another source of frustration. As discussed, between jail costs, program fines, court fines, and other factors, being poor in the criminal justice system is like pushing a boulder uphill. Defense lawyers do what they can, but when the people writing the laws do not care about helping the people who need it the most, our hands are often tied.

Good Days

As a defense lawyer, I have a lot more good days than bad days. Your goal as a defense lawyer should be the same. If you start having more bad days than good days, you need to figure out why this is happening. There are a number of things that can lead to a good day. Many of the things have nothing to do with a specific case or client.

Some days, a good day might just be spending time with a fellow defense lawyer and exchanging insights and stories about clients or judges. Belonging to a group of people who have so much in common is important. Some of my best memories over the past eight years are sitting around with defense lawyer friends sharing stories and laughing about them, learning from each other, and appreciating our role in the legal system.

Knowing that I belong to a cause that is fighting for something greater than ourselves makes many days incredibly rewarding. Fighting for a client that very few people care about gives defense lawyers a great sense of purpose, especially when the client is experiencing other difficulties because they are poor. I truly believe that if a person has a sense of purpose in his or her job, it is much easier to be happy.

Other great days that I remember have been after long difficult trials. Sometimes, it was a great day because I won, yet other days it might have been because I lost but I fought the good fight and the client appreciated the effort. On more than one occasion, a client has given me a hug after a guilty verdict. I have beaten myself up after a loss, but the client was actually the one telling me that I did a good job and that I should hold my head up.

Although defense lawyers should never judge their abilities solely on how their clients view them, it does feel good to know that the client understands that you went to bat for him or her and that you cared about his or her problem. As noted, many times our clients are poor and disenfranchised, yet they are the ones that need the most help.

Sometimes, a client's comments might make for a good day. Another time, a comment from a judge or a prosecutor might make you feel good about your work. Many prosecutors complimented me on something that I did. Sometimes, my action was small and seemed minor to me, but the prosecutor noticed it and said something. The action

might be as small as putting my arm around a scared client when a verdict is being read, or getting tissues for a
crying client. Positive comments from judges always make
for a good day.

When I was an intern at the public defender's office in
Ann Arbor, Michigan, I made a lot of appearances before
one judge who was known for being difficult and stand-
offish. Some of it was a character he was playing, but some
of it was actually him. I remember once during sentencing,
I was making some half-ridiculous argument on behalf of
my client. I did not really know what I was doing but I was
reaching for straws. After politely listening, the judge said
it was going to be clear that I would become a defense lawyer who was willing to fall on the sword for his clients. I
took that as a huge compliment. In those moments, I always
go back to the attorney who represented my parents.

Several years ago, I had a defense contract with a local
city court. My contract was not going to be renewed, which
was fine by me as I had lots of work. The judge I had been
assigned to was not pleased about it, however. The judge
wrote a three-page letter that she copied me onto, addressed
to the contract administrator about how unhappy she was
that she was losing me as one of her public defenders. She
went on to list all the good things she had come to expect
from me and how my absence would be a loss for the court.
She ended the letter by telling the contract administrator
that the defendants would suffer the most, as I was not

there to fight for their rights. Stuff like that makes you feel good about the work you are doing.

Just several months ago, I had one of the biggest honors of my career when a judge asked me to speak at his reappointment hearing. I have been assigned in this judge's courtroom for the last five years and have tried hundreds, if not thousands of cases in his courtroom. His reappointment hearing was coming up and because of political reasons, he was worried about getting reappointed. He asked a small number of defense lawyers to speak on his behalf to the city council. I was one of the lawyers he asked to speak. After I spoke and after he was reappointed, he was emotional and gave me a hug and thanked me for speaking. That was a good day.

Chapter Six

The People in the System

Everyone who is involved in the court system is a person, and—as we know—people are not perfect. I believe that everyone who I talk about in this chapter really does try their best. This is not to say I am naive and believe the system is perfect—far from it. The system can use many, many improvements, but I really do believe most people in the system try to do their best.

Judges

Judges are an interesting group of people. Just like everyone else who works in the system, there is a wide spectrum of judges and a wide spectrum of quality. If you ask a middle school student to describe a judge, he or she will probably say the following: "The judge is the smartest person in the room and only cares about justice and fairness. Judges do not have agendas and do not play politics." Unfortunately, the reality is often very different.

First, I have to talk about some of the amazing judges I get to appear before. There are judges who everyone likes, and these judges are unfortunately all too rare. A judge who is liked by the court staff, the prosecution, the defense lawyers, and the defendants is the ideal judge. There is no formula for what makes an excellent judge, but there are clear traits that I keep seeing over and over in judges that I consider to be excellent.

One of the most important attributes is patience. All the excellent judges I know are patient with everyone. A good judge will understand that if there is a new legal assistant or bailiff, he or she will need more time to figure things out. A good judge will also understand that if there is a new lawyer in the courtroom, the situation calls for patience. I have seen many judges who are not patient and quickly become angry or irritated when something takes longer than they think it should.

A good judge will also show patience with the defendants. Defendants may require a little bit of patience for a number of reasons. Many are scared and do not understand what is happening. A good judge will understand this and walk the defendant through the process. Some defendants have learning disabilities or brain injuries and may require more patience than others.

Another quality that excellent judges have is empathy. Having empathy does not mean that the judge is soft on crime or not willing to punish people for their crimes. Having empathy means that the judge can see where defendants are coming from and see what struggles defendants have had in their lives. When a judge has empathy, everyone in the courtroom can see it and appreciates it. I have seen many examples of judges showing empathy, but there is one example that sticks out in my mind.

The judge was taking a plea of a very prominent surgeon who was pleading guilty to a DUI. The judge followed the law and sentenced the doctor appropriately. What impressed me about the judge was that he told the defendant that he knew that his job was incredibly stressful and that he could see how someone could turn to alcohol to deal with the stress.

The judge said that he imagined that the surgeon dealt with incredible stress, holding people's lives in his hands, and how that stress must build up over time. The judge was not condoning that the surgeon had chosen to drink and drive, but the judge was showing empathy.

A good judge should also understand the law. Someone not involved in the legal system might assume that every judge has a mastery of the law. That assumption would be wrong. I have appeared before judges who were not just wrong about a legal issue, but they were totally out of the ball park. Many legal issues are very subtle, and it can be easy to see how two reasonable people might disagree. Some issues should be clear, and are clear to everyone except the judge. I have had a number of rulings where all I could do is turn my head and make a confused face. Part of the reason some judges are less knowledgeable about the law is because some judges have not had formal legal training and are not lawyers.

Sounds crazy right? Some states have a type of court called Justice of the Peace ("JP") courts. The courts go by different names in different places but are generally set up the same way. The judge is elected and is not required to be a licensed lawyer. All that this person is required to do to become the judge is win an election.

The courts are a holdover of an old system where there was a problem—lack of lawyers. It is hard to imagine now, but there used to be a time when there were not enough lawyers. Towns still needed judges, as there are always civil and criminal conflicts in society. At some point, someone decided it was better to have judges with no legal training than to not have judges at all, and the system was born.

This system made sense at the time, as the law was not nearly as complex as it is today. The judge just generally had to use common sense and try to figure out what was fair. Many of the towns that had these courts were tiny, and the judge did not have to rule on very many cases.

Today, the law is incredibly complex, and there is no shortage of lawyers, but we still have the JP courts. These courts make up a very small percentage of the entire system, but they are still there. Most of the cases go to city courts or county courts, but if you are a defendant in a JP court, you have a judge that is not required to have any legal training.

That being said, some of the JPs are excellent. They take the time to learn the law and become very good judges. I know some JPs who are better than some judges who have legal training. There are some JPs who are less than excellent. Some do not know the law and have no desire to learn. They rule over their courtroom and believe they can do whatever they want.

A friend of mine was at a JP court several years ago. The court was in an old conference room, and the defense and prosecution tables were folding picnic tables. The local JP pulled him aside and told him the following:

JP: "Boy, I know you're a big city lawyer and you like to file your big city motions. Let me make one thing clear, I don't want you filing any of your big city motions in my court."

My friend: "Uh, OK."

The JPs and their courts are in incredibly remote places and have virtually no oversight. Another friend of mine went to a different court in the most rural part of Arizona, and the local JP also owned the local gas station. The JP did not want to close down his gas station to hold court, so court was held inside the gas station. The JP cleared off the counter and told the defendant to start presenting his case.

Judges are people and people are imperfect. I have seen many judges whom calling "imperfect" would be a huge understatement. I have seen some truly terrible judges. I have seen judges intentionally insult and demean defendants who appear before them. Imagine how it feels to be standing in front of a judge who is supposed to be impartial and fair, and the judge is yelling at you, acting in a way that is the opposite of impartial and fair.

I have also seen my fair share of judges who have a clear bias for or against defense lawyers. Unfortunately, there are judges with whom you can guess correctly how they will rule on an issue just based on their personality. There are judges who will almost never find for the defense. This might be on evidentiary issues or on rulings of guilt or innocence. Oftentimes, when friends of mine tell me they are arguing an issue to a particular judge, I know what way that judge will rule.

In Arizona, some judges are elected and some are appointed. In both scenarios, politics can play a large role. If a judge knows that he or she is facing reelection, this could affect subsequent rulings. Some elected judges are able to stay independent, but some are not. The reality is that anyone who has to worry about winning an election or reelection will be aware of that fact—whether he or she wants to be or not. Arizona is generally a very conservative state, and, as you can guess, this comes into play when people vote for judges. Judges who are appointed face different dilemmas.

Judges who are appointed by a mayor or a city council have to first get appointed. To be appointed, they have to go through several interviews and get the approval of the committee members. If the committee is more liberal, it will likely appoint the more liberal candidates. If the committee is more conservative, this will also affect the choice. There are many political issues that intersect with criminal issues, such as drugs, prostitution, DUI, and other social issues.

Once a judge is appointed, he or she still has to worry about being reappointed every few years. If the committee or counsel or mayor is not happy with the judge, the judge can be removed off the bench. In reality, what this means is that someone can be an excellent judge but end up on the wrong side of city council and still lose his or her job. It would be great if judges did not have to worry about elections and appointments and could just exercise their own judgment with no outside influence. Some judges are able to do this and they are excellent judges, but some are not able to.

As with any profession, some judges are simply not very good at their job. I wish I could tell you that I have not seen a judge fall asleep on the bench, but that would be a lie. Some part of being a good judge is being efficient. Most courts are incredibly busy and if the judge is not efficient, the entire docket gets backed up. I have been in jail court and there were close to sixty people on the docket. The difference between an efficient judge and a non-efficient judge can be two extra hours in court for everyone.

Some judges are just unhappy people and carry their unhappy attitude with them onto the bench. I appear before some judges who are always in a bad mood. It does not matter the day, the time, or the occasion, but they are always in a bad mood. One of these judges was unhappy with me once because I came to court exactly two minutes late.

I know it was exactly two minutes because I remember looking at the clock as I walked in. He told me, "Around here, we start on time." I had a hearing with the same judge later that day, and he waited in his chamber for close to twenty minutes—just to make me wait. Talk about being passive–aggressive.

Prosecutors

I am different from some of my defense lawyer friends because I have prosecutor friends. I have defense lawyer friends who view prosecutors as enemies—no matter what. As I noted earlier in the book, I have one defense lawyer friend tell me once that she would never share a meal with prosecutors because they are "evil." Although I believe in our confrontational system and have no problem with going to battle with a prosecutor in trial, I believe that prosecutors have an important job to do—just like defense lawyers do. Having worked as a prosecutor, I know that prosecuting cases is not easy and that being a prosecutor comes with a certain amount of power over people.

A prosecutor can put a person in jail or prison; this power must not be taken lightly. All prosecutors are different, but just as with types of clients, there are several distinct types of prosecutors I often see.

Professional and Respectful Prosecutors—The Best of the Best

The first group is comprised of excellent prosecutors. These prosecutors do their job like they are supposed to. What I mean by this is that they seek fair outcomes and punish people when they need to be punished. This type of prosecutor has perspective, excellent judgment, and independence. This type of prosecutor knows when a harsh punishment is called for and when a defendant should be given a break. These prosecutors know that they carry a lot of power and do not abuse that power. Like Spider Man (borrowing from Voltaire) taught us, *with great power comes great responsibility.* I am fortunate to know and work with many of these excellent prosecutors.

One of the best examples of this type of prosecutor is a friend of mine who is now retired. I often worked with this person in jail court and he was an example of what a prosecutor should be. My friend was reasonable, fair, and empathetic all at once. If he could help a defendant, he would. He could tell when someone was a career criminal versus when someone made one mistake. He was a pleasure to work with because he not only looked out for the public but also for the defendants.

I have another friend whom I consider an excellent prosecutor. She is a pleasure to work with because she wants to come up with solutions that are fair to the victim and the defendant. She really cares about the people in court and actually wants to help them get back on the right track.

Another prosecutor friend of mine showed his true caring character outside of court. We would walk back from jail court and he would always give money to the homeless people we saw. He not only gave them money but also talked to them, treated them with respect, and even knew their names. Once he paid for one homeless man's cab ride to the Veteran Affairs Hospital so that he could get a refill of his medication. Unfortunately, not all prosecutors are this way, which leads me to the next type of prosecutor; some prosecutors are simply lazy.

Lazy Prosecutors

When you talk to them in court and ask them to check on something, they tell you they are busy even when it is clear they are not. These prosecutors are usually unprepared for trial—which is scary. I have spoken to prosecutors on the morning of a trial, and they had the wrong charges for my defendant. This is a small group but they are incredibly dangerous, considering how important their job is. Prosecutors are people and some people are lazy. As a defense lawyer, you must always be on the lookout for lazy prosecutors as they may cut corners or not notice something that could hurt your client. You are the last line of defense for your client and you have to make sure the prosecutor is doing everything he or she is supposed to in preserving justice.

True Believer Prosecutors

The next type of prosecutor is the true believer. The opposite of the true believer prosecutor is the true believer defense lawyer mentioned previously. The true believer prosecutors are incredibly dangerous and a huge threat to our system. For these people, every defendant is guilty. These people see the world as a very black and white place.

One way in which true believer prosecutors are dangerous is when it comes to charging a crime. Prosecutors can have a lot of leverage in how they charge a case. When charging prosecutors get a police report, they have to decide what charges to file. Prosecutors can choose to "hard charge" a case. What this means is that they will charge more serious charges than might be warranted. There are many examples, but a simple one may result from a bar fight.

There is an altercation and someone is stabbed. A prosecutor could charge that event as manslaughter or murder in the second degree. The difference in prison sentence can be significant. Hard charging can happen with pretty much any type of offense, including assault and vehicular crimes. Often true believer prosecutors are too friendly with the police and do what the police want them to do. Good prosecutors are supposed to use their own judgment and not let anyone else influence them.

One of the best examples of a true believer prosecutor involved a case that would be remembered as the "Donut Trial." Any trial that has its own title has to have a story and this one certainly did. The defendant had been charged with stealing one doughnut. The doughnut was valued at less than one dollar. The defendant was homeless and hungry, so he took the doughnut.

The prosecutor would not dismiss the charge. She said it was a matter of principle and that the defendant had to be prosecuted. She was asking for a ton of time in jail, so the defendant did not want to plead guilty. From his perspective, he did something wrong but he did not deserve to spend months in jail for stealing a doughnut. A trial was held, a jury had to be summoned and police had to be paid overtime. Imagine the cost of seven people missing a day's work and five officers paid overtime for the day since they had to testify. The defendent was found guilty and the judge suspended the sentence which means the defendent didn't have to serve any jail time or pay a fine.

I recently went to trial in which two homeless people were yelling at each other. They were alone in an alley and were not bothering anyone. My client, one of the homeless men, was charged with disorderly conduct. Again, I asked the prosecutor to dismiss the case and she would not because, in her eyes, a crime had been committed.

Dishonest Prosecutors

The last and arguably the most dangerous type of prosecutor is the type that lies. Again, I wish I had no examples of prosecutors lying, but that would not be true. I have seen prosecutors lie. There is one incident that stands out in my mind.

It was the morning of a nonjury trial and the prosecutor had to bring in a witness to proceed. I asked the prosecutor if her witness was present because I knew they had to have the witness. The prosecutor told me that the witness was present and in a back room with a victim advocate. I knew that this particular prosecutor had issues with honesty in the past, so I told her I needed to see the witness.

If it was a prosecutor I trusted, I would have taken her word, but reputation cuts both ways. The prosecutor told me that she was actually mistaken and the witness was not there. She said she misspoke. In reality, she had been caught in a lie. There is no easy answer as how to deal with a dishonest prosecutor. I would suggest bringing up the issue with the prosecutor first. If this does not resolve the issue, you may have to go to the prosecutor's supervisor or bring up the issue with the judge. Never accuse a prosecutor or another lawyer of something you cannot prove. You could mistakenly not only harm that person's reputation, but your own as well.

Court Staff

If you want a shortcut to ruin your career as a defense lawyer, be rude or disrespectful to court staff. I have one friend who has been working in the courts for many years. She still remembers a certain time that a defense lawyer was rude to her ten years ago, and she still tells me about it. I am always shocked when I see defense lawyers being rude to court staff. You would think that they would know better, but they do not. I always tell my law students that they should not only be nice to court staff because it is the right thing to do, but also because it is good for your reputation and your practice.

The court staff not only all talk to each other, but also to their judges and prosecutors and defense lawyers. Everyone talks and everyone loves gossip. Court staff such as bailiffs, clerks, and assistants can be incredibly helpful when you are nice to them. I have had countless hours of my time saved by court staff who were able to do small favors for me. If they know I am in a hurry, they can put my case on top of the file. The opposite is also true.

If I am rude to court staff, they can "accidentally" put my file on the bottom of the stack, and the judge will get to it in two hours. The reason that court staff can make a defense lawyer's job hard is because many of these people actually run their courts. An outsider would assume that the judge runs the courtroom, but this is not always the case.

I have been in more than a few courtrooms where the bailiff or clerk actually ran the court. They told the judge what to do and how to do it. The support people are also often in charge of arranging the files, so they decide what cases get heard and when. Sometimes, the judge was new and did not know what he or she was doing; other times, the judge was not new, but this was how their courtroom operated. A good judge will know that the support people can be incredibly helpful and make his or her own jobs easier.

Being nice to court staff can also mean making more money. I was working in a court in which I had a contract where I was paid per charge. This means that if a defendant has one file, I get paid once; if they have five, I get paid five times. I was talking to a bailiff in court, and she told me that they had a defendant with nine files and asked if I wanted the assignment. Taking on the cases resulted in several thousand dollars in my pocket.

Why did she help me out? There were two reasons. First, I have always been nice to her. Even when I am stressed or in a rush, I always make sure to be nice to her and the other court staff. Other defense lawyers may snap at her and not be polite. Second, I met with a relative of hers when that person had questions about going to law school. When she told me about her relative several months earlier, I told her I was a law school professor and would be glad to speak with her relative. She remembered me being nice to her and speaking to her relative, and she helped me out when she could. There are a million examples like this taking place in criminal courts every day.

Experts

Experts play an important role in the system. Experts are needed in many types of criminal cases; some of the most common issues that call for experts involve alcohol, forensics, accident reconstruction, and psychiatry. Generally, when people think of experts, they think of doctors and scientists, but many different types of people can be experts.

An expert is anyone who has expertise in a field. For example, in a case in which a car's brakes were at issue, a mechanic who does a lot of brake jobs can be an expert who testifies about the condition of the brakes. The experts I use in most of my cases are scientists who testify about blood alcohol concentration (BAC).

Since DUI cases are very technical, an expert is often needed for several reasons. First, to explain how the testing is done. Second, to explain if the testing was done correctly. Third, to explain what the test results mean. Most jurors have an idea of what a .08 BAC means, but—beyond that—they need help understanding it.

Another issue in which experts are often needed in DUI cases is to testify about BAC testing error rates. When blood alcohol is tested, it is generally tested through a big fancy machine that heats up the sample, and then it gets very technical from there. The machine, like all scientific machines and all scientific tests, has an error rate. The error rate can be important in DUI cases because it can be the difference between a defendant being over or under the legal limit.

In a typical case, a suspect will have a BAC that is close to the legal limit. The state's scientific expert will testify that the machine has a low error rate, normally five percent. The defendant's witness will testify that the error rate is a little higher and is ten percent. The difference might not sound like a lot but when you factor the five or ten percent into the BAC, it can be the difference between the person being over or under the limit.

Another way in which experts are used in DUI cases is as independent analyzers of the BAC. When a suspect has his or her blood drawn as part of a DUI investigation, two tubes of blood are taken. One tube is analyzed by the police crime lab. The second tube is kept so that the suspect can have the blood independently tested. If an expert analyzes the blood, the expert has to come to court and talk about the results. The results are usually close to what the government lab's results were—but again, a small difference can change the outcome of the case.

Experts can also be used in DUI cases to tell the jury if they think there was a problem with how the blood was analyzed in the government lab. DUI experts will look over the results from the government lab and determine if they think there was a problem.

Problems might include a contaminant in the lab or in the machine. Another problem could be human error and not using the machine correctly. Yet another problem that any DUI lawyer has seen is a mix-up with the vials. When the analysis is done, there is more than one sample that gets analyzed at one time. The machine can run anywhere from thirty to fifty samples at one time. If the machine thinks it is analyzing Person 1 but assigns the results to Person 2, there is a big problem.

As you can guess, not all experts are created equally. Some may be great at analyzing a problem on paper and explaining it to the defense lawyer but terrible at testifying. An expert who has to testify and is terrible at it is not very useful. If I have a brilliant expert who has every degree in the world but cannot talk to jury, that expert is not very useful. I use one expert exclusively in all my DUI cases.

I use this expert exclusively for two reasons. First, he is incredibly knowledgeable and probably knows more about BAC testing than anyone else in the state of Arizona. Although this is important, the second reason I use him is likely more important: Juries like him. He uses words they can understand. He breaks things down without being condescending or talking down to jurors. If a jury does not like your expert, they will be less likely to believe him or her.

As with defense lawyers, likeability will get you further than knowledge. I did a DUI trial with a newly hired government lab scientist testifying for the prosecutor. She was not very good at testifying and sounded awkward and unsure of herself. I had my usual expert witness who shot many holes in her testimony. The jury convicted my defendant, and I had the opportunity to talk to them afterward. The jury told me that it was clear my expert had more experience, but they believed the government expert because they liked her. They did not believe her because she was more knowledgeable or more experienced but because they liked her as a person. I learned a valuable lesson.

Private Investigators

A good defense lawyer must have a good investigator. Most good defense lawyers have several investigators. A good investigator can do many things that a defense lawyer cannot. One of the most important roles of an investigator is finding people who do not want to be found.

I will often have a case where I need a witness for that trial. The witness needs to be served with a subpoena, but the witness does not have a mailing address or I just do not know the mailing address. My client might give me the following info as to how I can find the witness:

> "If you go down to the bridge, and then walk a few hundred yards, there is a blue house. She used to live with a guy who lived next to the blue house with the dog with three legs. If you get to the other blue house, you went too far."

If I try to find that person on my own, the best-case scenario is that I won't find the person and the worst-case scenario is that someone is going to chase me with a knife. I cannot find the person based on that description, but my investigator can. Another very useful role of a good investigator is talking to the police.

Many private investigators are former police officers. In my experience, most of the good ones I have worked with are retired police officers. Former police officers know how to talk to current police officers. They not only know how to talk to them, but they also know how to get them to open up. When police officers talk to me, they will always have their guard up because I am the "bad guy", the defense lawyer. When police officers talk to a former cop, they will be more at ease and more likely to open up.

One of my investigators is a former Phoenix police officer, so he knows many of the current officers from his police days. I have had him help me with interviews in which the officers themselves had been previously trained by my investigator when he was a cop. Another time, I had a different investigator who was also a local police officer and who made quite a difference in local cooperation.

When my investigator, a former Phoenix police officer, was helping me with an interview of a cop he had formerly worked with, they actually caught up informally before the interview. They discussed kids, families, politics, officer gossip, and so on. After they were done catching up, the officer who was being interviewed was a lot more relaxed and talkative. I could not have done that without my investigator.

An investigator who used to be a police officer also knows how things are supposed to be done by the police and can tell you when someone screwed up. When I was new and did not know up from down, my investigator was invaluable because he pointed out a lot of mistakes police had made in my cases; I would have missed them on my own.

Juries

I was talking to a very experienced defense lawyer friend of mine about whether he liked to talk to juries after trials. He told me he did because of the following story. He had just finished a trial and decided to talk to the jury to figure out what they liked and did not like about his presentation of the case. One of the women from the jury who stayed behind told him that she was not sure if his client was guilty but decided to convict. My friend asked her why she did this, and she told him she convicted the defendant because she did not like the lawyer's shoes.

Juries are an interesting group. Most jurors try to do the right thing. Most jurors take their job very seriously and listen carefully. Most jurors weigh the evidence and decide who is credible and who is not. Sometimes, they ignore all of that and judge a case by the defense lawyer's shoes.

Sometimes, jurors fall asleep during the trial, and sometimes you can tell they are drawing on their notepad and not listening to a word.

For all the flaws of the jury system, I think the system of being judged by one's peers is a good one. Although everyone is entitled to a jury of the peers, not everyone's peers look the same. Ideally, every defendant would get a jury who looked like him or her. Young people would get young jurors; Latin defendants would get Latin jurors, and so on. In reality, when I have a minority defendant, the jury does not look like my defendant at all. I remember that I had a defendant who was a young African American male. He looked over at the jury, who consisted of all older white people and asked me if those were supposed to be his peers.

Part of a defense lawyer's job is selecting the best possible jury. The problem with this is that we can only pick jurors from the jury pool we are given. If there is a jury pool of fifty people, and they are all sixty years old and white and my defendant is a twenty-year-old African American kid, I have a limited choices.

Picking a jury is part art and part science. Some defense lawyers have entire complicated systems for selecting jurors. There are books, conferences, and systems that all claim to help you pick the best jury panel. The other end of the spectrum is pretty much picking jurors at random. I am not sure whether one approach has a higher success rate than the other.

When selecting jurors, you obviously want people who will be sympathetic to your client. Defense lawyers often know that convincing an entire jury is a long shot, so they just focus on one juror. If the jury cannot reach a unanimous verdict, there is a hung jury and the case is over. The prosecutor can re-file the charges, but this is at their discretion.

The science part of jury selection is trying to figure out what people might be sympathetic to your defendant and why. For example, if I have a case where there is some technical issue in the crime lab involving software and I am hanging my whole case on that issue, I want jurors with scientific backgrounds. I want scientists, engineers, and so on. Often, this thinking looks good on paper but goes down the drain in real life. Remember that you can plan all you want, but the best laid plans often do not work out. A good lawyer must be able to think on his or her feet and change course when it is called for.

The art part of selecting a jury has to deal with reading people and picking up on people's mood, vibes, and personalities. I had a DUI trial once and one of the potential jurors told the court that her husband had been killed in a DUI accident while he was in the Army. Her son had also been injured in a DUI accident. Conventional wisdom dictates that I run from this juror as fast as my little legs will carry me.

I stuck with the juror because she kept smiling at my young female defendant and said that my defendant reminded her of her granddaughter. I had a good feeling about the juror and kept her. My gut feeling paid off in part, as my defendant was acquitted of one charge and found guilty of a second charge.

Juries are also different from location to location and from town to town. I had a friend who was a public defender in the Los Angeles area. He told me that when he was doing a trial there, he could call the police liars and the jury would be okay with that. He told me that Arizona is different and that if he called the police liars here, it would turn off a jury.

If I am doing a trial in a more conservative part of Arizona, I have to take that into consideration, as I know that they will look at the case differently than a jury in a more liberal city might. Every defense lawyer knows which city is better for juries and which is worse. A good lawyer must be in tune with his or her jury pool and know what may turn him or her off.

I had a different defense lawyer friend who lived in Phoenix but did a lot of cases in northern Arizona. Much of northern Arizona is rural with many farmers and small town people. Whenever he had a trial up there, he made sure he dressed for the part. He would not wear the skinny ties and designer loafers that he would wear for a trial in Phoenix. Instead, he would wear cowboy boots and a bolo tie.

The Police

I thought a lot about what I wanted to put into this section. I knew I had to include this section because it would be impossible to write a book about the criminal defense world without addressing the police. Also, as I write this, there is a lot of discussion in our society about the police and issues relating to use of deadly force and racial profiling. The events of Ferguson, Missouri are still fresh in many people's minds. Like judges and lawyers, police make mistakes, and some police officers are good and some are bad. I have defense lawyer friends who think most cops lie and cheat. Overall, this has not been my experience.

First, the good news is that in my experience, most of the police I have dealt with have been honest and hard working. They do their jobs and they just want to go home. I have had many good conversations with cops about our jobs, our criminal justice system, and things that could be done to improve it. I have seen cops admit their mistakes and take responsibility when they were wrong. I have had more than one trial in which an officer was honest and said, "I didn't see what occurred." It would have been easy for them to say something otherwise, but their character and honesty were more important to them. I have seen prosecutors try to guide cops toward lying, and I have seen cops push back and stick to the truth.

I have also seen many cops cut people breaks. On countless occasions, I have had defendants who could have had their cars towed after a DUI arrest and impounded for one month, but the officers chose to cut them a break. An officer can sometimes have discretion on whether or not they impound a car. I have also seen cops cut people breaks on what charges they file against them.

I have also seen police officers use incredible restraint in their use of force. I have had defendants attack police and the police could have used deadly force but chose not to. It is easy to say cops should not use deadly force, but what would you do if a meth addict was running towards you with a knife?

Now, the bad news is that I have seen a lot of cops do terrible things. I think part of the reason people are so worried about out-of-control police more so than, say, out-of-control gardeners, is the power that the police have. The police can legally kill people. Think about that. We as a society have decided that we will entrust these people to keep us safe. We gave them weapons and let them make decisions on when to use those weapons.

One of the biggest problems I have seen with the police is lack of honesty. I have lost track on how many occasions I have seen officers lie on the stand while they are under oath. The really strange part is that they usually lie about something that does not even help the prosecutor. I have seen cops lie about some little things and some big things.

The problem with cops who lie is that it is almost always their word versus the defendant's. Generally, there is no audio or video recording, though this is swiftly evolving with technology among the police, defendants, and wit-nesses. What makes it worse is that there are usually sev-eral officers, and they all stick to the same story. Technology has made a huge impact here, as now there are more and more actions that are recorded.

Many police departments are now requiring body cam-eras for their officers. I think the cameras are good for every-one except dishonest police. The cameras are good for honest cops because the video will back up their stories. The video is good for defense lawyers because it makes our lives easier. If my suspect says he did not run from the cops, but the video clearly shows that he ran, there is little to argue about.

Body cameras have been one positive change, but cell phones have probably had the biggest impact on determin-ing what gets seen and what does not. Today, everyone has a cell phone, and every cell phone has a camera. It seems that everyone is recording everyone including the police. If a suspect is being beaten up by the police, a bystander with a cell phone camera can make all the difference in the world. The video tells the truth. If the suspect attacks the police and they have to defend themselves, that is one thing. If the police start beating up a suspect for no reason, this is a very different story.

Another major problem I have seen with some police officers is that they see the world as a black and white place. A person is either innocent or guilty. Much like how a child sees the world, they only see good and bad. I might have a defendant who stole food because he or she was hungry, but to some cops, a suspect stealing food for his family is no different from a suspect stealing electronics to sell them for drug money.

I often talk to cops in the court, as there is a lot of downtime. We wait for trials; we wait for defendants; we wait for judges. While we wait, we talk. I am sometimes shocked at how some of them see the world. I suspect, for some, it makes their job easier to see everything in its most basic, simple form. Although some cops are not very evolved in their thinking, some are outright irresponsible and dangerous.

I have seen many officers use excessive force and then lie about it. I have had cases during which independent witnesses will tell a very different story than the one an officer is testifying to. I have seen my clients with horrible injuries inflicted upon them by cops for no good reason. There is nothing more dangerous than a cop who enjoys power too much and takes out his or her anger on the citizens.

One of the worst types of cases I see involves the police picking on homeless people. I had a case several months ago in which a homeless defendant was charged with urban camping. Urban camping, despite sounding like a new X-Games event, is a type of crime in which the criminal justice system punishes the poor for being poor. The charge means that someone is living in a city park. Although I understand that we do not want parks filled with tents occupied by homeless people, they have to go somewhere.

My defendant was sleeping on a park bench. It was the middle of the day. There were no people around—no kids, nothing. My defendant was sleeping there because he had nowhere else to go. The defendant was not disturbing anyone or making a scene; he was just sleeping. The cop woke him and arrested him for urban camping. We had a trial because I was angry at the cop and my client was facing a hefty jail sentence for sleeping in the park. I asked the cop on the stand if he would have arrested someone for the same crime if he or she did not look homeless. The cop told me that he would arrest anyone for the same crime. I asked the cop if I went to the park in my suit, laid down on the bench, and took a nap, would he arrest me like he had arrested my homeless client. He told me yes, that he would have arrested me. It was clear that he was lying and only arrested my suspect because he was homeless but, despite my best efforts, my client was found guilty.

Another terrible thing I have seen police do is antagonize defendants who they know are unstable. I have had cases in which the police knew the defendant, knew the defendant was homeless and had mental health problems, yet the police would still provoke my defendant—just so that they could make an arrest. These police officers do a disservice to the community. They should not be cops.

Just as not all police are the same, not all police departments are the same. If you practice criminal defense long enough, you learn which departments are better trained and which ones hire better candidates. You also learn which departments hold their officers accountable. The scariest part is that you learn which departments have more bad cops who abuse their power. I will sometimes talk to cops, and they will tell me about a department that is notorious for police abuse or some other issue. If we lived in ideal world, all police departments would hold all their cops equally accountable, but that is not the world we live in.

Although corruption is an issue with the police, I think it is a very small one and an even smaller one when compared to other places in the world. Obviously, any amount of corruption by the police is not acceptable, but I know what real corruption looks like and we are doing fine.

I grew up in the former USSR; most of the cops there were corrupt and everyone knew it. The people knew how much they needed to bribe a cop to not get a ticket if they got pulled over. This is real systematic corruption that exists today in many parts of the world. Although I am sure there are a few officers who would accept a bribe, the vast majority would not.

Lastly, I acknowledge that the police have a difficult job. They generally see people at their worst. They see people who are angry, high, drunk, distraught, and sometimes dangerous. No one calls the police when everything is calm and everyone is being rational. That being said, it is a job that they signed up for. There is no mandatory draft for being a police officer. They took an oath to protect, serve, and defend. Lawyers work tirelessly every day to keep officers to their oath.

Chapter Seven

The Technical Side of Being a Defense Lawyer

Being a good defense lawyer means having many different skills. The first half of the skills needed is the personal side. The personal side means that a defense lawyer must be great with people, be great at marketing, be great at negotiating, have excellent communication skills, and be likeable. The second half of the skill set requires technical skills. This chapter addresses the main technical aspects of being a good defense lawyer.

Evidence

It is impossible to be a good defense lawyer without being a good trial lawyer. It is impossible to be a good trial lawyer without knowing about evidence. As important as understanding the rules of evidence is, you would think that all defense lawyers would take the time to learn them, but not all of them do. When I was a new defense lawyer,

I would be at trial and I was terrified that I would not know when to make an objection, or not know how to get some piece of evidence admitted.

I soon learned that as little as I knew about evidence, many of the lawyers I saw in trial knew a lot less than I did. Some prosecutors seemed to not know anything about evidence. I would often sit in court to watch other defense lawyers in trial. I soon realized, much to my horror, that many defense lawyers who had been practicing for decades knew very little about the rules of evidence. This led me to two realizations.

First, many judges do not have the best grasp on evidence. There have been countless times when I made a correct objection only to be overruled by the judge. More than once, I looked up the rule after the trial to see if I had been right only to learn that I had been. When I was in law school, I thought that every judge had a mastery of the rules of evidence. I was wrong.

Sooner or later, a defense lawyer will run into a judge who does not have the best grasp of the rules of evidence. There is no avoiding this reality. All you can do is stick to the rules as best you can. Make your objections and make sure you preserve issues on the record. "On the record" is the important part because doing this preserves any appeal issues. If you have a discussion with the judge in his or her chambers, this will not be preserved on the record and you could potentially lose an appeal issue. Remember, if it does not get said on the record, it never happened.

Always be polite when discussing an evidentiary issue with the judge. There is a difference between being firm and being rude. Having a bad attitude with a judge has never and will never help a situation. The chances you will change a judge's mind are very small. All that being said, judges who do not understand evidence are not the norm. Most judges I have come across have a solid understanding of evidence.

If you are not sure if you should make an objection, err on the side of making the objection. The worst thing that can happen is that the judge will tell you that you are wrong and the trial will move on. When making an objection, some judges will want to know the basis for the objection, whereas others are fine with just making an objection. You should always be able to explain why you are making the objection. If you are objecting and you do not know why, you have steered off course. I have seen some lawyers with laminated sheets that list every type of objection, and they bring these sheets to trial. The cheat sheet is not a bad idea, but you probably do not want your client or the prosecutor seeing it as he or she will assume you do not know anything about evidence.

The second thing I realized from watching other lawyers in trial is that every defense lawyer should put himself or herself through an evidence refresher course ever year or so. We all learned about evidence in law school, but this does not mean we cannot use a refresher. When I say a refresher, I do not mean memorize every rule like you do when you are studying for the bar exam. I mean that you should look through the rules and just make sure you remind yourself what the rules of evidence actually consist of.

The further you are from law school, the more you will start forgetting the rules of evidence. Ironically, the longer you are out of law school, the busier you become in your practice and you end up doing more and more trials, and you are thus presented with more situations pertaining to evidence. Being a good defense lawyer does not mean you need to be the greatest evidence authority, but it does mean knowing about the rules and knowing how and when to use them to your advantage.

Mentorship and Experience

If you want to learn how to be a good defense lawyer, you will need good mentors. It is impossible to learn the right way of doing things as a defense lawyer without having strong support from the right people who can show you the ropes. The reason that a new defense lawyer needs a good mentor is twofold. First, a mentor can teach the practice side of being a defense lawyer: what to do at trial, how to negotiate and plea, and when to file a certain motion. Second, a good mentor is needed to help young lawyers deal with the mental and emotional toll of being a defense lawyer. Having someone who has been around and has probably been through the same issues you might be facing is a crucial aspect to being a successful up-and-coming lawyer. Being a defense lawyer is complicated and difficult for many reasons. If you try to do it alone and without the help of mentors, you will most likely fail.

Many defense lawyers are fortunate to begin their careers at a public defender's office where there is a mentorship element built into the training. The mentorship program may be formal or informal, but there will usually be someone teaching you the right way of doing things. When I was at the public defender's office in Ann Arbor, Michigan, I was fortunate to have the benefit of a formal and informal mentorship program.

My formal mentorship program consisted of being assigned to an experienced defense lawyer who had been with the office for close to twenty years. This lawyer had been through every issue that you can imagine as a defense lawyer. He had seen and done everything you can do as a defense lawyer. I learned a lot from him about how to practice and how to carry myself as a defense lawyer. My informal mentorship program was less structured but just as valuable to me as a defense lawyer.

I would often have lunch, coffee, or beer with other defense lawyers in the public defender's office in which I was working as an intern. During conversations at informal meetings, I would learn a lot about what it meant to be a defense lawyer. The lawyers in that office had vast experience and were always willing to share information with me. I was only at the public defender's office for about three months but I know that I gained a grounding of information about being a defense lawyer.

What do you do if you are not at a public defender's office and need to find a mentor? This is the predicament I found myself in after moving to Arizona following law school. As I mentioned, I did not know any lawyers in the Phoenix area and had no one to turn to that could be a mentor for me. I did not know much, but I knew that I had to go where the lawyers were. I started going to as many lawyer networking events as I could. This was not difficult as I had no clients and no work, so I had a lot of free time on my hands.

I was at a new lawyer event and I chatted with a lawyer only a few years older than I was. He had been a prosecutor for about five years and had recently gone out on his own as a defense lawyer. After we talked for a while, I asked him if I could go to court with him to learn about the local courts. He was gracious with his time and said I could tag along. Maybe he thought that I would go to court with him once and he would never see me again. Much to his initial surprise, I started going to court with him every day.

He would drop his kids off at school in the morning and I would meet him at the school and then we would take his car to different courts. Those first several months that I spent with him saved my practice in two different but equally important ways. First, he taught me about the different local courts and how they worked. I did not know anything about local practice customs and he taught me everything I needed to know. He taught me about different prosecutors, judges, court programs, and everything else I needed to know to start my own practice.

Second, my mentor introduced me to many other lawyers, some of which went on to be important mentors to me later on in my practice. That one lawyer I met at the networking event introduced me to five or six people I consider mentors of mine. Without the help of that one lawyer and the other mentors, I do not think my practice would have succeeded. Find your mentors; they are out there and they are ready to help.

Plea Bargaining

Plea bargaining is an important part of the criminal justice system. When it comes to plea agreements, and the terms and specifics of the pleas, there are a million types with millions of different terms. Not only do different prosecutors' offices have different policies for plea agreements, sometimes even different prosecutors in the same office may offer a defense attorney different pleas. Like many parts of the criminal justice system, there is a science and an art component.

The science component is knowing enough about a case to understand if the plea you are being offered is a good plea, or at least a reasonable one. When a prosecutor gives you a plea bargain, you have to be able to tell if the offer you are being given is reasonable, fair, and advantageous to your client. One of the main factors in determining the answer to these questions lies in determining the strength of the prosecutor's case. Part of the science analysis is determining the likelihood of winning at trial versus the consequences of losing at trial.

I recently had a case in which my client had used a stolen credit card to buy roughly seventy thousand dollars worth of goods. The state had a very strong case against my client and I knew the likelihood of losing at trial was very high. Part of the job of a defense lawyer is explaining this analysis to the client. Another aspect of analyzing the strengths and weaknesses of a plea offer is the jail or prison consequences of losing at trial.

In city court, the potential risk of going to trial is usually relatively small. A plea offer may call for ten days jail but you, as the defense lawyer, know that if your client loses at trial, the judge is likely to impose the same ten days of jail. In cases like this, the potential exposure to the client is fairly small. Felony cases are often very different. In a felony case, a plea offer may have ten years of prison but if your client loses at trial, he or she could expose themselves to twenty years of prison or even more. All this goes back to the scientific analysis of looking at the plea offer in relation to the prosecution's case and the likely outcome of a trial. The problem with a scientific approach is that trials, and criminal defense practice, are not a science. This is what brings us to the artistic aspect of plea bargaining.

There is a certain art to getting a good plea offer from the prosecutor. Good defense lawyers will practice this art and refine it after years and years of practice. Part of this goes back to people skills. This may sound obvious, but if you are nice to the prosecutor, they are more likely to give a better offer. Part of the art is also developing relationships with prosecutors. As mentioned, the criminal law world is small. Defense lawyers tend to run into the same prosecutors over and over. If a prosecutor knows you as a defense lawyer, and knows you are reasonable when you ask for something, he or she is more likely to listen.

Another aspect of the art of plea bargaining is creativity. Oftentimes, a good defense lawyer may be able to craft a creative solution that maybe the prosecutor had not thought of. This might include letting the defendant plea to a different charge, or working out some kind of creative sentence that is a good outcome for the defendant and leaves the prosecutor satisfied that justice was served. Be creative when coming up with possible resolutions to the case. The worst thing that the prosecutor can say is no, and then you have not lost anything.

Trials

Trial work may be the single most defining and difficult part of a defense lawyer's work. One of the things that distinguishes defense lawyers from all other lawyers is how often defense lawyers are in trial and how much trial practice they accumulate over their career. I have spoken to many civil lawyers who have never gone to trial in their entire career. I have talked to more than one civil lawyer who thinks of jury trials as something more out of a John Grisham novel than as part of his or her own practice. Contrast this with most criminal defense lawyers.

It is impossible to be a defense lawyer and not go to trial. Obviously, your caseload and the type of cases you are handling will dictate how often you are in trial, but there will be many trials. I have had days in which I had four non-jury trials in one day. I have also had weeks where I had two separate jury trials in the same week. I do not have an exact count, but I would guess that I have anywhere from twenty to forty various trails in any given year. I have defense lawyer friends who make my trial numbers look like child's play. I have friends who do court-appointed felony defense work and they seem to be in trial every single week. I have friends who often need motions to continue one major trial as another trial is running long.

The length of trials varies greatly. Misdemeanor trials can last from an hour to several days. The shortest trial I ever had lasted only several minutes as the state only called one witness and only asked this person several questions. I had no questions for that witness and had no witnesses of my own. Felony trials can vary from several days to many months. A good friend of mine had a felony murder case in which the state was asking for the death penalty last over one year.

Seeing as defense lawyers are often in trial, it should be obvious that a good defense lawyer needs to be comfortable with trial work. The best way to become comfortable with trial work is to do lots of trials. There is no substitute for repetition. Trial work is no different from any other skill. If you want to be good at playing the violin, you have to play the violin. If you want to be good at trial work, you need to do trials. The question always becomes, how do you handle trials when you are a new defense lawyer and do not have any experience?

The answer is that you should fake it until you make it. Everyone starts out as a new defense lawyer with no experience. At one point, the greatest criminal defense lawyer in the world had zero trials under his or her belt. Remember this when you stand up in front of a jury for the first time. When you stand up in front a jury for the first time, your stomach may be in knots, and you may feel like you are going to throw up, but you have to act like it is no big deal and pretend that you have done this a million times before. Remember, if you panic, how do you think your client will feel? If you freak out, how much confidence will your client have in you?

I will never forget my first jury trial. It was a DUI case and I was terrified. Unlike many defense lawyers, I never received any formal trial work training. I did not have the benefit of working at a public defender or prosecutor's office where I would have received extensive trial work training. I was terrified and I remember being scared that my client would ask me how many jury trials I had done before. I would have given her the honest answer and she would have been rightly scared. No one wants their surgeon telling him or her that he or she has never done surgery before.

One good thing to remember is that, generally, the court will cut you more slack in trial when they know you are new. Remember, at one point the judge and the prosecutor were also new. In my experience, as long as you are nice and professional to the judge and the prosecutor, they will help you as much as they can. Being humble and respectful has gotten me out of more jams in trial than I can count. That being said, everyone will still expect you to be prepared and no one will do your work for you. This brings us to our next point.

There are many variables of a trial that you cannot control. The one that you can control is how prepared you are. There is no excuse for not being prepared for the trial. Being unprepared makes you look bad to the judge, the prosecutor, and, most of all, to your client.

Being prepared is not only important from the viewpoint of putting yourself in the best chance of winning the trial, but also from protecting yourself professionally. You do not want to be explaining to your state bar why you showed up to trial unprepared. Again, no one expects you to win every trial, but everyone will expect you to be prepared.

There are many things that go into being prepared and one of the most important and often overlooked is knowing your opposing counsel. If you have a trial coming up with a prosecutor you do not know, you need to get as much information about this person as possible. How are they in trial? What is their trial style like? Are they known for trying to play tricks in trial? Are they considered honest and trustworthy? These are just some of the questions you should try finding answers to. These questions are important and the answer will also help you determine your own affective trial strategy.

One good way to learn about the prosecutor handling your case is to talk to other defense lawyers. Talk to as many lawyers as you can who know that prosecutor and have been in trial with him or her. The more information you have going into trial, the better-off you will be.

Appeals

Appeals is an area of criminal defense in which lawyers seem to either love or hate the work. Some lawyers find appellate work to be dry, boring, and lacking all the elements of the criminal defense work that they enjoy. Other defense lawyers enjoy appellate work as they do not have to interact with clients much and often get to work on novel and new legal concepts. There are several things all defense lawyers should keep in mind when it comes to appeals.

Always remember to make a record to preserve issues for appeal. You may be in trial with a terrible judge who is violating every law and every rule, but if you do not make a good record of your objections, they will be lost. For example, you go back to the judge's chambers to have a discussion. None of what you say will be on the record, which means it does not exist for appeal purposes. No matter what, you have to get your issue on the record so it can be preserved. On a related note, do not ever say anything on the record that you do not want an appellate judge to hear.

Also remember that being a good appellate lawyer is a skill just like any part of being a lawyer. When I handled my first appeal, I was scared and did not know what to do. Now I have done a large number of appeals and feel a lot more comfortable with the type of work. I am still not as comfortable with appeals as I am with trials because I have done more trials than appeals. If you are having a hard time with your first appeal, do not get discouraged.

Chapter Eight

Advice from Those Who Have Been There

One of the best parts about being a defense lawyer is that you belong to a unique community of people who can relate to the struggles and joys of being a defense lawyer. Defense lawyer communities are small because defense lawyers make up a small part of the larger lawyer community. As a result of this, most defense lawyer communities are closely knit and people look out for each other. Defense lawyers are always there to help a fellow defense lawyer. I know that when I have a question, I can turn to my defense lawyer friends and they will do everything they can to help. Every defense lawyer I know takes pride in helping new defense lawyers. Every defense lawyer remembers how stressful and terrifying it is when you are a new defense lawyer.

This chapter is a result of speaking to experienced defense lawyers and asking them what they would tell new defense lawyers. This chapter is also about what experienced lawyers wish they knew when they were brand-new defense lawyers. The advice in this chapter comes from lawyers with varying degrees of experience. The years of experience range from ten years to over fifty years.

This too Shall Pass

I recently had an issue in which I was worried about losing a very lucrative contract. Long story short, I had a very difficult, unreasonable court-appointed client who was complaining about me to everyone who would listen. Even though I know I had done everything correctly and ethically, the defendant was still complaining to everyone from judges to court administrators. All of this was going on during the time of year when our annual contracts with the court were up for renewal.

Reasonably, or not, I was worried that because of the defendant's complaining, my contract may not be renewed. The contract in question was a good slice of my income and losing it would be a big hit to my practice. I had the contract for five years, but renewals were never guaranteed so I was worried. I ran into the presiding judge at the court and he could tell that something was on my mind, so he invited me into his chambers to talk. I told him the situation and he gave me some of the best advice I had ever gotten as a lawyer.

The judge is now in his seventies and has been on the bench for over twenty years. Before being the presiding judge in this court, he was a long-serving judge in a different court. Before being a judge, he spent several decades as a defense lawyer handling all kinds of criminal matters. He had a wealth of experience as a defense lawyer, so he understood the many challenges faced by defense lawyers when dealing with difficult clients.

The judge told me that when you get to his age, you realize that many of the things that seem like huge problems are actually nothing to worry about. He told me that looking back on his long career, he spent a lot of time worrying about things that never amounted to anything. This really resonated with me as I have a habit of worrying about things.

Ultimately, what the judge said would happen did happen: absolutely nothing. I was renewed for another year without a hiccup in the process. I had spent all that time worrying about what could happen as a result of the defendant's complaints and nothing happened. If I had spent no time worrying, everything would have turned out the same and I would have saved myself a lot of worrying.

When I look back on my last years of being a defense lawyer, I can think of many times when I spent a lot of hours and days worrying about things that amounted to nothing. I think of all the hours I spent worrying about terrible possibilities that never materialized. Being a defense lawyer means you will have hardships and difficulties. This is an absolute truth that must be accepted. What is important is how you deal with the issues that come up. You can either drive yourself crazy worrying about what could happen, or you can realize that bumps in the road are all part of the journey and go on with your career and your life.

A good analogy for worrying about career problems is worrying about relationships in high school. Remember when you were in high school, or maybe college, and you had a boyfriend or girlfriend, and fights with that person seemed like matters of life and death. I remember that I had a long-term girlfriend in high school and every time we broke up, I thought the world would stop spinning. Looking back on it now, it is funny. When you look back on those relationships, was the worrying worth it? Chances are high that you do not even talk to that person anymore. The same thing happens with many of your problems. One day, you will look back and realize that the worrying was not worth it.

The Obstacle Is the Path

"The obstacle is the path" is an ancient Zen proverb. I do not remember who told it to me, but it I often think about it in the context of being a defense lawyer. Being a defense lawyer has always been difficult work, and will always be difficult work. It is stressful and challenging on a normal day. What makes being a defense lawyer enjoyable and rewarding is also what makes it challenging. If the job was easy and had no stress, how rewarding would it be? This idea applies to any job, or any endeavor for that matter. How rewarding would it be for a brain surgeon if the work was not incredibly difficult and lives were not at stake?

How rewarding would winning an Olympic gold medal be if it did not take a lifetime of sacrifice, training, focus, and dedication to win? Everything that is rewarding is difficult. Think of your own biggest accomplishment in your life so far, and I guarantee that it took a lot of work, dedication, and effort to accomplish it.

Being a defense lawyer is rewarding because it is difficult. If you go into a career as a defense lawyer hoping for an easy road, I have bad news for you. If you go into knowing that it will be difficult but embrace the challenge, you will make it easier on yourself. We know enough about human nature at this point to know that people are happier when they have purposes and goals. Think of how often you hear of people battling depression as soon as they retire. When a person retires, this person often loses his or her purpose, which was his or her work. Being a defense lawyer is more than a job; it is a purpose. Embrace the hardships and know that they are what make a career worth having.

Develop Relationships

It is virtually impossible to succeed in the practice of law without being able to build relationships. Every aspect of your professional life will depend on your ability to build and cultivate relationships. One area of being a criminal defense lawyer in which building relationships is crucial is with prospective and current clients. Why would prospective clients hire you if they do not think they can build a relationship with you?

When you are meeting with a prospective client, or a new court-appointed client, you have to be able to start building a relationship in which the client knows that you are trying to help him or her, and are on his or her side. If a new client does not think that you care about him or her, your life will be more difficult. In general, the longer you work with a particular client, the more of a relationship you build. I have had countless court-appointed clients who were outright hostile when I first met them. Some of them had bad experiences with previous defense lawyers, whereas others were simply difficult people.

With these clients, I can usually track their change in attitude as they warm up to me and begin to trust me. The change does not happen overnight. The client may trust me five or ten percent more each time we meet, but the relationship grows over time. This is not always the case. Some of your clients will never trust you and you will not have much of a relationship. Your goal is to try to build relationships with your clients where you can.

Another area in which relationships are crucial for defense lawyers is when it comes to other lawyers. Having good working relationships with other defense lawyers, prosecutors, and judges will make your life a lot easier and happier. I cannot tell you how important it is for me to have defense lawyers in my life who I know I can turn to for help. Although a defense lawyer being able to turn to other defense lawyers might be expected, there are seemingly odd places that I often turn to for advice. I am friends with several prosecutors and will go to them for advice on occasion. Sometimes, it might be a procedural question about how a certain court handles a type of case. Other times, it might be a question about how they might handle an aspect of a case. Too many defense lawyers think of prosecutors as the enemy without considering that they can be a great source of information.

I also have excellent working relationships with several judges. On more than one occasion, I have turned to friends of mine who are judges for career and life advice. Most of lawyer-judges have decades more of practice experience then I do and can be a wealth of information for me. In turn, I have had several judges ask me to write letters of recommendations for them for various positions they have applied for. I have also had the same judges write letters of recommendations for me in the past several years.

Remember that building relationships with clients and fellow lawyers takes time. The prosecutors and judges that I reference have known me for years. We did not develop relationships overnight. Do not try to force deep trusting relationships after knowing a prosecutor for only a week or a month. Do what you can to cultivate the relationships.

Ask people out for lunch or coffee. If you have not talked to a fellow lawyer for five years, how much of a relationship is there in the first place?

Having these relationships will prove incredibly helpful in times when you need help, and I promise you that there will be times when you need help. Sometimes, the help you need will have to do with the law and sometimes it will be more of a personal matter. As I have mentioned, being a defense lawyer is difficult. Having people around you to talk to will help you immensely. Start building relationships on your first day and those relationships will make all the difference for you down the road.

Take Care: Protect Yourself and Your License

Being a defense lawyer is stressful and difficult. I have said it before and I will say it again. As a result of the stress, many lawyers develop unhealthy relationships with alcohol, drugs, and food. Too many defense lawyers end up not taking care of their health and some end up paying with their lives. In my eight years of practice, I have known a handful of defense lawyers who died too young as a result of not taking care of their health.

Weight gain lead to serious medical issues for some of the lawyers I know. With others, it was chronic health issues from alcohol or drugs. What they all have in common is that they did not take care of themselves. They convinced themselves that they were too busy to go for a walk, go to the gym, or eat healthy. I hear so many of my colleagues say that they wish they had time to work out, but they are too busy with work and other obligations. Too many lawyers ignore the advice of their doctors to lower their cholesterol and blood pressure. This is the wrong attitude. Your own health and well-being must come before your career. What is the sense of building an incredibly successful practice if you are too sick to enjoy it? What is the sense of working so hard that you neglect your health and then you end up not being around for your family?

I had a mentor and friend die several years shy of his fortieth birthday. He had a thriving practice, was making lots of money, and things were going incredibly well. He had a wife and small kids. Everything he did was for his wife and kids so that they could have a great life. He worked insane hours and kept a crazy schedule. He also neglected his health. He gained a lot of weight and never spent any time on his own physical and emotional well-being. He got sick, and because his body was already worn down, he ended up dying. I was incredibly close with him and losing him reminded me about the importance of taking care of myself. Several months before he died, we had lunch and he told me about how he was looking forward to slowing down and spending more time with his wife and kids.

Another part of taking care of yourself is taking care of your license. As a lawyer, your license should mean everything to you. It is your meal ticket, and your way of providing a living for yourself and your family. I do not even like to think of what my life would be like if I lost my law license. It should go without saying that as a lawyer, you must do everything to protect your license but too many lawyers make bad decisions that lead to the loss of their license.

After eight years of practice, I personally know six lawyers who have been disbarred. All of them made really bad decisions. These decisions had very little to do with substantive law and more to do with good judgment. Several of these lawyers had substance abuse issues that clouded their judgment. This goes back to the importance of taking care of your health. One of the lawyers was tired of practicing, burnt out, and he made choices that I suspect he knew would lead to his disbarment. Several of the lawyers ran into financial hardship and made terrible choices with their own money, and, worse yet, with their clients' money.

When I teach Professional Responsibility, students are always terrified that they will make one small mistake and get disbarred. In reality, getting disbarred is not easy to do. I have known lawyers to make very major mistakes and receive punishments short of disbarment such as probation or classes. As long as you take care of yourself and take care of your license by making good decisions, you will be fine.

The Job Will Not Save You

"The job will not save you."

—Lester Freamon, The Wire

The quote is from one of my favorite TV shows of all time. One of the main characters of the show is an alcoholic cop named Jimmy. Jimmy is divorced and is kind of a hot mess. The only thing that Jimmy has in his life is his work. Too many defense lawyers are like Jimmy. I know too many lawyers who only have their jobs. Their entire lives focus around their jobs. They forgo vacations and family time to spend more time working. Some work too much because they are trying to help their clients; others do it to make an extra dollar. There is nothing wrong with working hard and pushing yourself. It is, in fact, the only way to build a successful career. It becomes a problem when the only thing you have in your life is your job.

The job will not save you. If all you have in your life is your job, you will never be happy. The things that will make you happy are things such as family, friends, and hobbies. The key, like with every aspect of life, is balance. If you spend every hour of your life working, this is a problem. If you do the opposite and spend no hours of your life working, this is also a problem. The happiest lawyers I know are the ones who have found balance between their careers and their lives away from work.

You have to make time to do things that you enjoy outside of work. For some lawyers, this is their families and kids. For some lawyers, it is volunteering or traveling. My wife and I enjoy traveling and take several large trips per year, and a decent number of short trips as well. At this point in my career, traveling is difficult because I have to be in court every day. I could say I do not have time to travel because I am too busy, but then I would be choosing my work over my life outside of work. Instead, I spend a lot of time planning court dates around the days when I will be gone.

Many of my lawyer friends who would like to travel more but are worried about leaving work tell me that I am lucky that I get to travel as much as I want. What they do not realize is that it is not luck. I make getting away from work to spend time with my wife a priority. As the old saying goes, when something is a priority you will make time, when something is not a priority, you will make excuses. What you do outside of work does not matter. What does matter is that you are not in your office twenty-four hours a day.

I also know many lawyers who only have their jobs and they are not a happy bunch. These lawyers are often divorced or never got married. They generally have very few interests outside of work and pretty much all they talk about is work. I can run into them at a party and all they want to talk about is work or some new court decision that just came out. I want to talk about football and they want to talk about appellate law. This is not a happy bunch of lawyers and every time I am around them, I am reminded that the job will not save me.

Plan Ahead

I believe that one of the main differences between lawyers who have happy careers and the ones who hate their jobs and end up burnt out and unhappy is how much planning an individual lawyer does. There are two main types of planning that will make you a happy lawyer. The first type of planning is career planning.

Career planning involves thinking about where you want your career to be in five or ten or twenty years. This does not mean that you make a rigid plan that you cannot deviate from. What it does mean is that you think long term about where you want your profession to be down the road. In my experience, the most successful lawyers make plans and then work on achieving them. Conversely, lawyers who do not have successful careers tend to just go with the flow and lack solid plans.

When I decided to write my first book, I was a young lawyer and had no experience in the writing and publishing world. I knew that becoming a commercially successful writer would take a long time. I made small goals of where I wanted my writing career to be in one-, five-, or ten-year increments. Doing this gave me goals to work toward. If I would have said my goal is to be a commercially successful writer, this would have been too vague. What does that mean? Small goals have involved things such as having a publishing deal with a publisher I wanted to work with, or being on the Amazon.com top seller list for legal books.

Think about where you want your career to be in five or ten years. Do you want to have your own practice? Do you want to have a certain number of county or city contracts? Do you want to have an assistant or an associate? Do you want to be able to take five or six weeks off every year to write to travel? The more questions you ask yourself and the more you plan how you will accomplish these goals, the better-off you will be.

The second type of planning is financial planning. I am always amazed at just how many defense lawyers I know have little or no financial plan. Having a financial plan is not just for lawyers in private practice. If you work for a government agency, planning your financial future is just as important. Planning your financial future is no different than planning your professional future. You need to ask yourself a lot of questions and then figure out a game plan.

Ask yourself questions like:

- When you want to retire?
- What does retirement look like for you? Will you work part time or not at all?
- How much will you need savings if you want to stop working?
- How much money do you have saved in case of an emergency?

- How long can you stay in practice if you have a bad financial run and you have no new clients coming in?
- Are you spending money on things you do not need?
- Where could you change how you spend money?

My long-term financial plan has always been to strive for a point where I could afford to not work. I do not ever see myself not working, but I want to know that I have that choice. To me, real wealth is being able to do what I want when I want. I still have a long way to go before I get to my goal, but the important thing is that I have a goal and a plan and I know what I am working for. For some people, their financial goal is a fancy house or a fancy car that they can show off. I think these goals are short-sighted, but that is not the point. Again, what is important is that you have a financial goal and a plan for how you will get there.

Chapter Nine

Making a Difference

Every day, defense lawyers go to work and fight for people's rights. The government has the ability to put people in cages and to even execute people. Defense lawyers are a check on the government's power. This is a huge responsibility, but also one of the most rewarding parts of the system. Everyone says he or she wants to protect the Constitution, but how many people actually get to do it as part of their job? Every time a defense lawyer exposes police, prosecutorial, or judicial misconduct or any other wrongdoing, the defense lawyer is protecting the constitution.

Only Criminals Need Defense Lawyers, Right?

Many people do not like defense lawyers until they need one. I often hear people tell me that they could never be defense lawyers because defense lawyers only defend guilty people. Although many of my clients are guilty of the crime for which they are accused, what happens if an innocent person is charged?

Brandon Mayfield was arrested for an act of terrorism. The FBI had linked him to the deadly Madrid, Spain bombing that had killed one hundred and ninety-one people. The FBI said they had a one hundred percent positive fingerprint link between Mr. Mayfield and the bombing site. Mr. Mayfield was arrested and held without charges for two weeks. He described his two-week detention as hellish. The only problem was that Mr. Mayfield had nothing do with the bombing, and he was later be exonerated of all charges. The FBI offered a formal apology to Mr. Mayfield and agreed to a two million-dollar settlement. Without defense lawyers, Mr. Mayfield could have been put in a cage for the rest of his life. This is why defense lawyers are important.

It would be nice to think that instances like this are insanely rare and innocent people are never charged, but unfortunately this is not true. Today, the Innocence Project lists three hundred and twenty-nine defendants in thirty-seven states who have been freed through DNA testing (www.innocenceproject.org).

Think about that number. There are over three hundred people, many of whom were incarcerated for murders they did not commit. Something else to think about is if three hundred and twenty noninnocent people have been freed, how many more innocent people are in prison today? How many have been executed? Imagine sitting in a cage for the rest of your life knowing that you were innocent. It was not politicians, prosecutors, judges, or the police who saved three hundred and twenty-nine lives. Defense lawyers saved those lives.

How Can You Defend Those People?

Not all our clients are good people and some of them do unimaginable, horrible things. Some of our clients have very little humanity left in them. Defense lawyers who are honest with themselves will acknowledge this, but we also have clients who are good people who just made a mistake. Oftentimes, defense lawyers play a huge role in shaping the outcome of that person's life.

I had a client who was a college student; he got too drunk at a basketball game. His friends dared him to pull his pants down. He did and one of the security guards at the game saw him. The student was arrested and charged with indecent exposure. The prosecutor wanted the student to be registered as a sex offender. Having to register would have ruined this kid's life. He would never be able to find a place to live or a job.

Although pulling one's pants down at a basketball game is dumb, it should not ruin the rest of one's life. I was able to get him a fine and no registration. This is one of the millions of examples that take place every day, and this is how defense lawyers help people. Every day, defense lawyers fight for people who need it the most. I think that is my favorite part of the job and why I am proud to tell people I am a defense lawyer.

The truth is that poverty and class play a huge role in our criminal justice system. Poverty and class play a huge part in every aspect of our society, so why would they not play a huge role in the justice system. If you go into a county jail or prison, you will see that most people there grew up poor with very few opportunities. This is not groundbreaking news. Many books have been written on the interplay of crime and class in the United States. Defense lawyers alone cannot fix the monumental problem of poverty and its effect on crime, but they can try to balance the scales. A defense lawyer fights for the clients no matter regardless of economic status. Defense lawyers protect everyone's rights. Sometimes, the right we are protecting can be as simple as someone's ability to go to work.

Most of the time, the initial effect a defense lawyer can have might seem minor while actually making a huge difference to a defendant. There are countless times when I have a defendant who is in custody on a nominal bond. The bond may be fifty or one hundred dollars. To a lot of people, this is an insignificant amount that they could easily pay. For many of my clients, one hundred dollars might as well be one million dollars.

Many of my defendants who end in custody have jobs but after paying all their bills, they literally have nothing left over. Many of them are also in custody for old fines or tickets. If they are in custody, they cannot work. If they cannot work, they lose their jobs and are even worse off than before. When I can convince a judge to release my defendant without a bond, the defendant is able to go back to work and keep his or her job. It is not an exaggeration that many of my clients end up homeless if they lose their job as they have no support system.

Be an Agent of Change

We can all agree that there are many problems that we face as a society. Many of these problems are deep rooted and do not have simple answers. Although most people like to simply complain and throw their hands up in frustration, defense lawyers have a unique opportunity to actually make some positive changes. Defense lawyers can do their part to bring about change in several crucial ways.

One of the most important roles of a defense lawyer is to defend the Constitution. Every time a defense lawyer files a motion challenging a bad stop or a bad search, the Fourth Amendment is being protected. Every time a defense lawyer appeals an unjust lower court decision, the rights guaranteed to all of us are being protected. This is incredibly important.

I really do believe that defense lawyers are one of the last lines of defense for protecting the Constitution and the Bill of Rights. Defense lawyers do and must continue to serve as a check on the government's power. I like knowing that when a police officer is about to pull someone over, the officer is aware that he or she may have to answer for his or her actions to a defense lawyer in courtroom one day. This is an important and vital check on the police and the government.

A defense lawyer has the chance to fight injustice every day. How many professions have that kind of opportunity? Whether the injustice is a poor person being charged, jail costs they can never afford, or a young person being harassed because of the color of his or her skin, there is no shortage of work for a defense lawyer trying to do good. I see defense lawyers do amazing work every day to protect the most vulnerable members of society.

I have one defense lawyer friend whose entire practice revolves around helping defendants with mental health issues and learning disabilities. She works tirelessly to keep them out of jail and to make sure they get the mental and medical help that they often desperately need. In her career, she has helped thousands of defendants, all of whom were better-off because she cared about them and wanted to help them. There are countless examples of defense lawyers like this.

At the end of the day, we all have a choice to make. We can say the problems of society are too big, too daunting, and we simply cannot fix them all on our own. Or we can say that we cannot fix all the problems but we can each do small parts and help where we can. As defense lawyers, we have a unique and special opportunity to be agents of change for the people we represent. Through our work, we can alter the trajectory of our client's lives in meaningful and amazing ways.

Chapter Ten

Conclusions

The Winds of Change

The entire legal profession is changing. Some of the same changes are also taking place in the criminal defense world. Some of the changes are good. Technology has transformed how defense lawyers are able to practice. Today, I run my entire practice on a laptop and a cell phone.

Today, my law students could not imagine a world without being able to look up any case in the world online. Looking up a case twenty years ago meant going to a library and pulling a book off a shelf. Once you found the book, you had to hope the case law was still relevant, as the book was published at least a year ago. Technology has transformed countless parts of the legal profession.

Fifteen years ago, this would not have been possible. The changes have made it possible for smart lawyers to keep their overhead down and earn more money. Today, a lawyer can use a second cell phone or a call-answering service for a fraction of the cost of a full-time assistant.

Another good change is that the criminal defense and criminal justice communities have become more diverse. Although there is always room for more diversity, we are headed in the right direction. Being a lawyer used to be a white man's profession; this is changing quickly. More and more women and minorities are becoming judges, opening their own practices, and taking on leadership roles within their organizations. I know that out of all the judges I appear before, more than half are women. Fifty years ago, close to one hundred percent of these judges would have been white men.

Although there are some good changes, there are also some bad ones. Today, a defense lawyer has to work harder than ever to be successful. There are more lawyers, which leads to more competition than ever before. As discussed, more and more people are fighting over smaller and smaller pieces of the pie. Lawyers are not only now competing with other lawyers, but with document prep companies and websites that claim that to provide all the necessary forms, so people do not have to "waste" money on lawyers. The good part about more competition is that it forces the smart lawyers to advance and evolve their practices. There will always be room for lawyers to succeed if they are creative and hard working.

Another upcoming change on the horizon is less and less funding for full-time and contract public defenders. As cities and counties continue to struggle with their own budgets, there will continue to be more and more budget cuts in public defender programs. If a politician or a bureaucrat cuts the funding of a public defender's office, this person knows that most voters will not protest much. To the general public, all that public defenders do is defend criminals.

Having worked some of these contracts myself, I know that they have been cut and continue to be cut. Oftentimes, the lawyers who have the contracts are classified as independent contractors, which means that we do not have very much negotiating power. The issue simply comes down to supply and demand. There is a greater supply of lawyers looking for contracts than there are contracts. This means that contract administrators can go to defense lawyers and say, "Take it or leave it because I have two hundred people applying for your position." I am not exaggerating with the large number of applicants. When I was awarded a contract several years ago, I was told by the contract administrator that over two hundred other lawyers had also applied.

Another unfortunate change that has been creeping up for some time now is the diminishment of the Bill of Rights and the Fourth Amendment. It seems like every year some court makes a decision that chips away at people's liberties. Many of these decisions are made under the cover of either national security or fighting terrorism. These decisions take away law abiding people's rights. Today, people know that their phones are being tapped and conversations are being recorded, but we are told this is necessary for national security reasons.

As police and prosecutors are given more and more leeway and power, the job of the defense lawyer becomes harder and harder. I am optimistic that this change will stop and that courts will start protecting people's rights. The Bill of Rights and the Constitution were things that made this country so great and unique.

Just as that public defender helped my parents when they were immigrants who were new to the United States, I hope that I have tried to carry on with the crucial work done by defense lawyers every day. I truly believe that defense lawyers are one of the last lines of defense in protecting people's rights and the rights guaranteed to every person in the Constitution. My hope is that new lawyers and law students will continue to carry on with this work so that future generations are protected. The work of defense lawyers is difficult but rewarding—challenging but crucial. There is no job I would rather have.